STARVING IN THE SHADOW OF PLENTY

STARVING
IN THE
SHADOW OF
PLENTY

LORETTA SCHWARTZ-NOBEL

Authors Choice Press
San Jose New York Lincoln Shanghai

Starving in the Shadow of Plenty

Authors Choice Press
an imprint of iUniverse.com, Inc.

For information address:
iUniverse.com, Inc.
5220 S 16th, Ste. 200
Lincoln, NE 68512
www.iuniverse.com

Originally published by G.P. Putnam Sons

This study was prepared under the auspices of the *Plymouth Institute*, a nonprofit social and political policy analysis organization located in Plymouth Meeting, Pennsylvania.

Portions of Chapyter 7 appeared in different form in *Ms. Magazine*, October 1979.

The text of this book was phototypeset in 11 point Century Schoolbook type at the Plymouth Institute.

ISBN: 0-595-18566-5

Printed in the United States of America

This book is dedicated to the memory of Martha Roca, and to all the other people in this country who have died hungry and alone, in the hope that this kind of needless suffering will also die.

Contents

Acknowledgments

Many people helped me create this book, more than I can name here, although the final responsibility for its accuracy and validity remains with me. I received assistance and encouragement from Gregg Trahey, Linda Wengel, Phyllis Young, Marcellus Lloyd, Cindy Hansberry, Denise Rambo, Helen Driscoll, Richard Frye, Joe and Lisa Gmuca, Bertha Scurry, and Joe Koprich.

I'd especially like to thank my husband, Dr. Joel Nobel, whose love and strength and support sustained me through all the difficult times. Also, Alan Halpern for believing in this work enough to publish my first article on hunger, and for his invaluable guidance in shaping this book.

Michael Pakenham, associate editor of the *Philadelphia Inquirer*, whose idea it was that I write a book on hunger and whose efforts over many years helped to make it possible.

Kay Traylor for her devotion and indispensable help in typing more than a dozen manuscript drafts. This book is also hers.

My father and mother, Abraham and Fay Rosenberg, who never tired of reading those drafts.

My stepchildren Josh and Erika Nobel for their cooperation; my daughter Ruth for her encouragement; and my daughter Rebekah, who not only went with me to visit some of the people in this book but also helped me to understand and write about them.

Ellen Levine, my literary agent, for her excellent judgment.

And my fine editor, Faith Sale, under whose wise guidance this book was formed.

Finally, I can never adequately thank the people whose lives are depicted in these pages for talking to me, for taking me into their homes, and for trusting me.

I
The Problem Now

Man can hardly even recognize the devils of his own creation.

—Albert Schweitzer

1 The Reasons for Hunger

The only thing necessary for the triumph of evil is for good men to do nothing.

—Edmund Burke

I found her by accident, trying to crawl out of her doorway and down the broken concrete steps in an effort to get food. She was eighty-four and living alone in what looked like an abandoned house near the corner of Ninth and Bainbridge streets in South Philadelphia, less than a mile away from my comfortable town house. On her head was a small crocheted cap. Once, long ago when her husband was alive and she could still walk, she had taught crocheting. Her name was Martha Roca. She had almost starved to death.

That afternoon in 1974 I went with my seven-year-old daughter Rebekah to our local supermarket and bought food for Mrs. Roca. In the months that followed it became our habit to take several bags of groceries to her each Saturday afternoon. Rebekah thought of it as the best part of our week. There was something in the experience of giving that moved and delighted her. When Martha Roca laughed with tears streaming down her face, saying, "Thank you, thank you, darling dear, when I feel better I'll crochet," Rebekah felt her joy and believed we were solving the problem. But by then I had met Julia, who also lived nearby.

Down a narrow alley where renovated and dilapidated houses stood side by side, Julia, whose weight had dropped from 150 down to 90 pounds, was sitting in her doorway on a torn green plastic chair and hoping, as she always did, that someone would visit her. She was wearing the dark blue dress that she usually wore—the better of the only two she owned. Julia peered up at me from the darkness of her room. Then she smiled. She had no teeth, and her toes peeked through the holes in her straw slippers. She invited me in, and I sat down on the couch where she slept. I felt something on my leg. Automatically I went to brush it off, and then I saw them—hundreds of roaches running across the filthy green-and-white linoleum, over the fading flowered wallpaper, across the biblical scenic calendar and the postcard smile of John Cardinal Krol, archbishop of the Philadelphia diocese. Everywhere. Even if there had been any food in Julia's kitchen the roaches would have consumed it before she could.

Julia didn't see or hear too well, which was

probably a blessing. Wanting to be hospitable to me, she raised her arm and pointed to a faded photograph of herself and her family. She, young and plump at twenty-one. Around her neck was a silver crucifix.

"I am High Episcopalian. I was christened in Camden [New Jersey] on June 28, 1899. There's no one left but me," she said sadly, "so I know God left me here for some purpose."

I couldn't help wondering exactly what purpose it was that God had in mind for her.

"Do you get much food? Do people go to the store and get you food?" I asked, seeing how thin she was.

Her voice cracked. "No," she said sadly, "there ain't been nobody around at all."

Once, on a Saturday, she had tried to go to a local supermarket, but she tripped and fell in the gutter. She lay there for a long time before a little boy stopped and helped her up. She tried once again, on a Tuesday. That time she got to the store and managed to buy a few things, but on the way home someone grabbed the bag of groceries and ran away. After that she was afraid even to try, so she sat there on her torn green chair among the roaches, waiting for the guests who never came and waiting also, rather patiently, for God to let her know the special purpose He had in mind for her.

I knew that Rebekah and I could add Julia to our list and take her food on Saturdays along with Mrs. Roca. We could help them, but I had done some research and had learned that there were tens of thousands of other people—men, women, and children—in Philadelphia alone who were desperate for food.

They were America's hidden poor, forgotten in

the midst of our prosperity. They had been identified by the government; they were represented by statistics stored in government computers and filed in government cabinets. They were among those President Lyndon Johnson had intended to include when he declared his War on Poverty ten years earlier in 1964.

But the Johnson administration had failed to redeem its promises to the hungry and poor, and in 1969, Richard Burns, one of Nixon's top domestic advisers, had confidently announced that poverty was only "an intellectual concept defined by artificial statistics."

In November 1974 I had accidentally encountered some of the faces behind those "artificial" statistics and I had glimpsed the anguish and the human suffering that they represented. What I saw had changed my vision of America. When I returned to the main streets of Philadelphia and watched people in expensive restaurants, laughing, sipping cocktails, and eating lobster at noon, I felt certain they were unaware that their neighbors were starving.

For years I had been unaware, and so had the director of public relations for The Philadelphia Corporation for Aging whom I contacted for guidance. She told me that she had lived in Philadelphia almost all her life, and that she was dumbfounded to find little alleys in South Philadelphia with one- and two-room shacks. She had explained that old people, mostly white, lived in these places, sometimes without heat or water or gas or food and that these people were extremely isolated. Often the people who needed help most had no radios or TV sets to hear public-service announcements. Even if they did, many of them didn't have phones, or sometimes they were simply afraid to call.

At her suggestion, I rode in the van that delivered the free lunches made available by the Corporation for Aging, a federally funded program which exists in part to feed poverty-level senior citizens one-third of their minimum daily food requirement. That's when I met Eddie.

As we drove, Joanne Schwartz, the nutrition program director at the Albert Einstein Medical Center, explained to me that she was taking food to an old woman down the street when a man rushed out of his house and told her he was afraid Eddie would die. Actually, Eddie had a sister, but she lived in the Northeast and didn't see him. Most of the people who received the lunches were in that situation—either they had no families or they had been forgotten by them, left behind.

We parked in a South Philadelphia Italian neighborhood, walked to the end of a block of old but neatly kept row houses, and knocked on the door of what appeared to be a boarded-up corner store.

Eddie was sitting on the bed, where he spent most of his time. That was because he couldn't walk or dress himself or even go the bathroom alone. So he sat there, his emaciated legs dangling uselessly over the side of a sheet that hadn't been changed in months. Flies walked on the soiled bedspread that covered him; empty peanut tins, dirty cups, and used paper towels surrounded him. His thin blond hair fell in wisps across his high forehead, touching the large, silver-rimmed glasses that framed his finely chiseled face. His upper lip quivered, and his body tensed with excitement as he saw us. Eddie was not an old man. He was only thirty-eight. That, I was to learn, was one of his problems.

"Hi," he said, raising one arm and then letting his paralyzed hand drop against his bare chest, "it's so good to see you."

Eddie lived with Tim, an elderly and senile uncle whom he loved and tried to care for. But Eddie, who weighed only seventy-four pounds, needed care himself. Together they built the only world they could. For the most part it was a world that depended on the kindness of others. Sometimes a neighbor would come and carry Eddie to the bathroom or open one of the cans of food that the Department of Welfare homemaker brought when she visited once a week.

"Tell me what that homemaker does," Joanne whispered. "Look at this place and tell me what she does!"

I looked. It was impossible to tell what color the linoleum had been because the layers of grease and dirt were so thick. The table where Eddie's Uncle Tim ate looked as if it hadn't been cleared in weeks. Eddie said he had food in the cupboard, but, because he had no way of getting to it or using a can opener, he ate only on occasions like this, or when a neighbor came. Recently he had spent two weeks in a hospital. It was the first time in years that he had eaten three meals a day and slept in a clean bed.

Joanne handed Eddie one of the five lunches he would receive that week. He looked at the salad, chicken, and gelatin, but he didn't begin to eat. He knew I was there for some reason, and a visitor is a big event when your world is as limited as Eddie's.

We talked a little, and then, his voice a high whisper, Eddie said, "I'm so grateful for all that's been done for me." I assumed he meant the lunches, since it didn't look as if anything else had ever been done.

16

Just before I left I noticed that a large, framed painting of a white-robed Christ with arms uplifted in blessing hung above the metal bed, and I understood that for Eddie, and many other people I was to meet who had suffered greatly, deep religious faith was a form of sustenance.

Actually, Eddie's survival depended on another kind of sustenance, the free lunches made available by the Corporation for Aging. But, at thirty-eight, Eddie wasn't a senior citizen and Joanne was not supposed to be feeding him.

However, Joanne wasn't taking any chances. She tried that once. She had been delivering food to an old man on Winton Street in South Philadelphia. She'd also been giving lunches to his wife, who was younger than the program mandated. The man suddenly disappeared and the wife wouldn't tell her where he went; she became very uncooperative and sullen. Joanne got bureaucratic and stopped bringing her lunches. Five days later the woman was dead.

There were twenty-five other stops on that route, the agency delivered one meal a day, five days a week. Those five meals were all that most of the people ate each week. Nobody knew how many hundreds or thousands of other people in that area of Philadelphia were starving. From that perspective, I knew that Eddie was one of the lucky ones.

I began to investigate hunger in Philadelphia. Contacting federal and private agencies, I found that the federal government had cut back the previous year's allocation to the Philadelphia Corporation for Aging. The corporation had been functioning for about eight months. Because of the critical nature of the nutrition problem in this country, the federal government had given it top priority under the Older Americans Act. The initial program consisted of setting up a series of lunchrooms in the city's poorer neighborhoods.

The day the feeding sites opened, many of the people who came kept their backs turned because they were putting food in their pockets to take home for dinner: They were still trying to get more food when all the food was gone.

The thirteen sites that had been established soon became so overcrowded that most were turning people away. However, the one I visited at 6600 Bustleton Avenue in Northeast Philadelphia fed everyone—although they all ate less. "You can always thin the soup and we have plenty of extra bread," explained the director. The food designed to take care of a hundred people was feeding two hundred, and the nutritional supplement was only one-sixth of the adult minimum daily requirement. But that was better than nothing, so they came.

Many at the Bustleton site were Eastern European Jewish immigrants who had arrived around the turn of the century—hungry then, too, but filled with dreams of streets paved with gold, of private enterprise, and freedom from want and hunger. They were proud, gentle people who didn't need much anymore; still, they needed something. Many were living on Social Security checks that were as low as $91.60 a month, an amount that wouldn't have been enough to survive on in 1960, let alone in the inflated economy of the mid-1970s.

They sat at card tables, the men usually dressed in suits and ties, the women in print dresses. They insisted on sharing their food with me—a little spaghetti, a hamburger thinned with meal, and a few mixed vegetables. Not fancy, but kosher—an important requirement for people who had always lived by the Book.

I asked one little old man if he had anything to

eat at home for dinner. He shrugged. "I'm a light eater; this is plenty for me. And I'll tell you—if you have your dedication to the Torah, you always have spiritual food."

Some of these people were escapees from Nazi Germany, people long familiar with the ravages of hunger. One must understand that, to know why no one would ever be denied food at the Bustleton Avenue site. One family of survivors that was once very prominent in Vienna—two sisters, a brother, and their mother—ate there. Once the director asked the brother if he would like to stay late for a special men's program. He told her that he would not stay without his sisters and his mother—since the war they had never left one another alone.

Despite the dedication of the staff, there were a lot of people who were very hungry. The site had to be closed for two weeks that fall; some meals were delivered, but not everyone could be fed. There were four deaths during those two weeks.

Weekends, too, were empty times. Most of the people were lonely as well as hungry; for some of them, mealtime at the site was a chance to meet other people, and to socialize. But on weekends, only a few of the luckiest ones visited relatives. One man went to a local cafeteria to enjoy the good smells and the crowds, but he couldn't afford to buy much.

On the afternoon of my first visit I met a frail, tiny old lady named Leah, immaculately dressed with a black shawl wrapped around her shoulders and a pair of old black, orthopedic shoes on her feet. Before eating, Leah removed a small plastic jar from her purse. She was trembling—a condition that, I learned, never left her—and she had difficulty unscrewing the top of the jar. Finally she opened it. Leah carefully put exactly half of her spaghetti, half of her hamburger, and half of her vegetables into it. On this night she would have dinner.

Leah told me that when she came to the United States she worked for many years in a factory. Now she received Social Security: $104 a month, of which $75 went to pay her rent. She was left with less than a dollar a day to live on. So when she said she was a light eater, I wasn't surprised.

All the time we spoke, Leah held my hand—held it tightly, in a way that said she was hungry for more than food. And when we said good-bye, she kissed me, saying, "Come again, God bless you. God bless America." Then she apologized profusely for not having better English, better hearing, and better eyesight.

I wrote an article about the people and the conditions I found, and it was published in the Christmas issue of *Philadelphia* magazine. The article shocked the city. Almost instantly offers of money, food, and clothing flooded the offices of the magazine.

A few months later I went to Washington to accept the Robert F. Kennedy Journalism Award for the article, and as Ethel Kennedy handed me a bronze bust of her husband inscribed *For Outstanding Coverage of the Problems of the Disadvantaged*, I looked out at the audience of senators, congressmen, and journalists. I wanted to tell them that I hadn't "covered" the problem, that I had just barely begun to *uncover* it. I wanted them to know that there were people like Martha Roca and Julia and Eddie and Leah all over America, but Ethel Kennedy was shaking my hand and congratulating me and all the senators and congressmen and journalists were clapping. Then it was time to sit down.

Shortly after I returned home I was confronted with a personal shock. My marriage of fourteen years was over. Suddenly my own security seemed to crumble. My children and I had to find a less expensive place to live. That meant a poorer and possibly more dangerous part of the city. The conditions of the people whose lives I had written about suddenly seemed less distant from my own. I was starting to understand how fragile each of our "secure" positions is.

I had seen a few of the individual casualties of a society that had become so committed to growth at any cost that it failed to take care of its most helpless members. I was still several years away from grasping the nature of the real American dilemma.

I did not know yet that comfortable, well-fed Americans could themselves someday become victims of the same indifference and greed and blindness and the same political and economic dishonesty that had caused hunger among their neighbors.

Nor did I realize that the poverty and starvation I had seen were just one manifestation of a national poverty, a poverty of judgment, which had already begun to undermine the foundations of America.

For the first time, however, I began to feel personally vulnerable and to wonder if I would have enough money for food for my children and myself. Despite that concern—or perhaps partly because of it—I started to direct more and more of my energy toward learning about the problems of the hungry.

I began to travel to the hovels and back alleys of other American cities, finding the hungry, speaking to experts, and publishing investigative reports. I did this in Boston, Chicago, and Washington, as well as in Philadelphia.

Returning to Washington after receiving the award, I quickly learned that thousands in the nation's capital were without adequate food. Some of the District of Columbia's poor were living on cheap, inadequate, mostly starch diets, so it was not surprising to find even obese children who were dangerously undernourished.

I met one young mother of five who was living in a single room at the top of a brownstone on N Street in Northwest D.C.; she explained proudly that she used to run out of food all the time, but did better now because she didn't buy any meat or fruit.

I looked at her children, aged four, five, seven, eight, and nine, sitting almost too quietly on the floor in the darkened room. One little girl smiled at me shyly.

"What do the children eat?" I asked.

"Rice," she answered. "They never complain as long as I cook enough rice to fill them up."

Hunger did not stop at the District line. Inside the large, white, nine-story Presidential Building on Belcrest Road in Hyattsville, Maryland, the lines for food-stamp certification started forming at 4:30 a.m. Despite the fact that no posters or signs directed people to the proper office and no information was posted about the necessary qualifications, they came in droves. Many waited all day without food and went home without hope of getting any. The food-stamp program was set up by the Department of Agriculture, so that qualified low-income residents could be given a subsidy to buy more food and upgrade their diets. Unfortunately, it doesn't often work that way.

At 6:00 a.m. one Monday I sat down in one of those stiff, straight-backed wooden chairs designed for those who must wait, and I began to talk to the people around me. Several explained that they had called before coming and had been told that they would have to wait six weeks for an appointment, or come at 5:00 a.m. and hope to be seen in a "free moment."

A young woman who sat staring off into space wiped her eyes with the back of her hand. Her lips were trembling. She had arrived at 4:30. "They want my husband to sign this support slip," she said, holding a form in her hand.

"Does he support you?" someone asked.

"Oh, no," she said, "he disappeared a few weeks ago. He was living with his girlfriend, but then he moved out. I told them I couldn't find him, and they said, 'Okay, we'll give you an extension; we'll give you more time to find him.' But I promised my kids I'd come home with food today—they haven't eaten anything since yesterday morning."

She didn't have to tell us how long ago yesterday morning was to children who had eaten no food since then. Another woman sitting nearby added quickly that she thought the children would be all right because for three or four days every month her children walked around the house asking when they were going to get some food. "But my children know what the story is. They are used to it," the woman said. "They know that we have to wait till we have more food stamps.

"At Easter time I wanted to buy the children new shoes. I knew it would mean I couldn't buy as much food that month, but I wanted it very much. All their shoes were broken and torn. You can understand, I am not fancy, I just don't want my kids to be the laughingstock of the neighborhood, even if it means they have to eat less. For myself, it doesn't matter. I don't care if I'm in worn-out rags with no decent shoes. I don't have any place to go. My time is over. I had my day when I was young and married.

He was a truck driver. He told me if I'd hop on that truck and leave my mother I'd be with him. I'd be his wife and he'd take care of me forever. Well, he stayed a couple of years—a real handsome man, a wanderer, I guess. One morning I woke and he was gone. Now, I just keep trying to stretch the money, but no matter how hard I try, for a few days at the end of the month we just have to do without."

Some people I met "did without" for so long that deprivation became the expected way of life. Others arrived here from abroad believing that life in America would be better than what they had fled from.

Lawrence and Nancy Rongione and their ten children never had much, even in Puerto Rico, but when floods came and destroyed their hut, Lawrence Rongione sold the family's only remaining possession—a car— and with the money brought his family to Boston.

Soon afterward, a teacher noticed that the Rongione children were coming to school sick, sleepy, and starving.

An investigation revealed that, except for the free lunches they were eating in school, the children had eaten no food for a month and a half. The entire family was living as squatters in the Mission Hill housing project in an abandoned apartment without plumbing or heat.

Racial strife between blacks and Puerto Ricans and the desperation of drug addicts made the project dangerous even during the day. Olga Santiago, a social worker who had been held at knife point a few weeks earlier, bravely guided me over the glass of broken windows, past graffiti-covered brick walls and the angry stares of lonely men, into the hallways reeking of urine and filled with garbage, up to the second-floor tenement where the Rongione family stood waiting.

They greeted us, the father nodding silently. The mother, a tired-looking woman missing her upper teeth, was surrounded by children of all sizes. All were barefoot except for a boy of about ten who wore shoes that were too big, without socks; most of the children had sores on their faces and bodies, and all of them had colds.

The Boston Housing Court had just given the family three weeks to get out of the project.

"Where will you go?" Olga asked in Spanish.

"We do not know," the mother replied. "No one will have us. I feel like leaving this place and flying away. I am desolate. I do not find happiness in anything here.

"There was a small check from the Welfare Department," Mrs. Rongione explained. "So the first week of the month, we had food, mostly white rice and kidney beans. But by the next weekend the food and the money were gone. Right now," she said, putting her arms around her six-year-old daughter, "we are out of food and have borrowed all we can from the local store."

Outside, it was already getting dark, and the sounds of the street were growing louder. As I walked away from the tenement, I looked back at the Rongiones' apartment and saw three little girls, leaning through the sharp, jagged edges of the broken windows, waving good-bye and throwing kisses.

Much as Americans would like to think of these men, women, and children as incompetent, ill-favored, and weak, or as inhabitants of isolated pockets of poverty, the truth is that many have a strength and a tenacity, and an ability to endure hardships, that their more fortunate neighbors never develop.

I spent much of the next four years exploring the experiences of the hungry. I found that hunger in America was gathering momentum. Thirty million Americans were living below the federally established poverty level—of $3,790 a year—and my experience suggested that most of these people were hungry. Statistics indicated that the numbers were increasing.

Anyone who doubts that hunger in this country is increasing needs only to look at our vanishing natural resources, our rising cost of food, the fixed incomes of our elderly, and the proposed cuts in programs of federal aid.

President Reagan maintains that the "truly deserving and needy" will be spared from his budget cutting but that is not the case. The fact is that Reagan's plan for a "new beginning" will mean the end for millions of Americans. It promises to create massive increases in hunger not only among the traditionally poor but among the unemployed, the lower middle class and the elderly now living on fixed incomes. The decontrol of oil has raised the price of fuel and food still higher. Millions who have traditionally had enough to get by will now have to choose between food and heat. If we continue on our present course, those thirty million poor and hungry Americans will only be the first wave of victims of an impending national disaster.

In fact, many of the people who are hungry today were not always poor. Some were doctors, teachers, or other kinds of professionals who had fallen between the cracks of the Social Security system. Others with special needs found survival on small fixed incomes nearly impossible.

This is the story of those Americans, but it is also the story of the rest of us, for hunger will not remain in the traditionally troubled areas. Already small towns and farms all across this country are finding themselves with few economic options.

Still, when the possibility of widespread hunger in America is predicted, disbelief is the dominant response. Despite the fact that this nation has the highest unemployment rate in the industrial world, many Americans think it couldn't happen in *their* neighborhoods or to *their* families. Most people still know little or nothing about the extent of hunger in America. No comprehensive study of malnutrition has ever been made.

To many Americans the image of a starving child is still just a distant cliche'. They think starvation is something that happens in other countries—Idi Amin's Uganda, or Mother Teresa's India. America has long been known as the breadbasket of the world: Who could starve here where we have the highest food production per capita ever known?

Certainly, it is thought, America has enough food for all of its people. But we forget that to a lesser degree so does the world. Today the world could feed 5.2 billion people. That is 800 million more than the highest estimate for the world's population. Even in the worst years of famine there was plenty of food. Hunger is not simply the result of scarcity or poverty. Energy shortages, inflation, the destruction of vital farmland, the failure of crops to respond to chemicals, problems of food distribution, and the mismanagement of food production all affect food supply and increase food prices. Evidence of an emerging pattern of dislocation is everywhere.

Supermarket food prices rose an average of 14.5 percent in the twelve months preceding June 1, 1978, according to a survey taken by newspaper food editors in seventeen American cities. Double-digit inflation continued to rise through 1979. During the first nine months of 1980 prices rose another 9.5 percent. By November even the conservative Department of Agriculture had predicted that food prices would continue to rise throughout 1981.

In order to understand why the cost of food kept increasing in the United States, it is necessary to look at the factors that affect it: the food production system and the food distribution system, the energy and fuel requirements necessary to run the agricultural equipment, and the reliability of the chemicals used to increase crop yields.

The information I accumulated while doing this research led me toward conclusions that at first were hard for me to accept. I had always assumed that there was little or no connection between the very old or poor people I had seen starving in America and the problems or shortages or attitudes that might cause the middle class to experience hunger. But it turned out that there was a vital connection. It had to do with the values that many Americans had *stopped* cherishing.

The American philosophy was based on the belief that there was more of everything than people would ever need. Both resources and individuals became expendable. Many policymakers thought only of the present. They became careless and damaged many things that did not need to be damaged. They mistreated land and energy sources just as they had mistreated people. When land that had not been well cared for could no longer produce, it was simply sold or forgotten and new land was

28

cultivated. When oil wells ran low, they were deserted and other wells were drilled. When people became old or worn out and could no longer serve as part of the traditional American work force, they, too, were abandoned.

Often these discarded people were not respected in any way or given an opportunity to teach the younger generations about the things that they had learned or believed in, frequently the very things that had made this country strong. Many were packed away in nursing homes. Some were provided with Social Security that kept them alive but did not give them enough to live decently. In the process, a number of the simple traditional values that had bound American people and families together were destroyed. Most Americans still maintained their formal religious affiliations, but many lost their true sense of reverence. They forgot how to be caretakers.

The changes in attitudes and in values affected families and personal lives, but they also also affected policy decisions that were being made at every level. As the quest for money, at any cost, increased, big business and big government also increased. The country became more compartment-alized. The connections between individual abuses and larger patterns became more and more difficult to see. Business leaders and legislators did not seem to understand the crises that were developing or the ways that they were converging.

As a result, in the 1970s a rapid succession of problems began to surface. The country seemed to be running out of everything at once—energy sources, topsoil, cropland, and food reserves—while inflation and demand for these resources continued to in-crease. By 1980 the situation had grown even worse. The individual shortages and failures actually foreshadowed problems that had been building for years. The general public had remained largely unaware that the ground was shifting beneath them because the policymakers had continued to cover shortage after reported shortage with short-term solutions, gimmicks, and unrealistic promises.

Our political leaders were often well-intentioned and honest, but they had failed to understand that America's agricultural infrastructure was being undermined by thousands of careless piecemeal decisions, controlled by interests of the moment, which were often in conflict with each other and with long-term needs. Gradually, and painfully, a few of our politicians came to recognize the connections between the rising cost of food, the oil shortages, the land abuse, large corporate interests, and the agricultural vulnerabilities which they had wrought.

The Carter administration constantly revised its forecasts of inflation, food price increases, and energy shortages upwards, but in its preoccupation with short-term economic indicators, it did nothing to prevent the continued misuse of our natural resources or the continued depletion of the ecological foundation of our economic system—the croplands, fisheries, and grasslands—which provide all of our food.

One day in my reading I came across a statement made by Lester R. Brown, president of the Worldwatch Institute, a nonprofit organization that analyzes global problems. Brown's concept had nothing to do with the suffering of individual hungry people and yet it seemed to tie everything together. Brown suggested that America was experiencing "the economic signs of ecological stress." He said that the first symptoms are physical—deteriorating grasslands, shrinking forests, and soil erosion. At the next level, stresses manifest themselves in economic terms—scarcity, inflation, unemployment, and economic stagnation or decline. And, finally, the stresses assume a social or political character—hunger, forced migration to the cities, deteriorating living standards, and political unrest.

I believe that America has already experienced the first two phases that Brown described and that it is rapidly entering the third. The Reagan administration inherited these problems. It is looking for ways to solve them. But it is making choices that ignore the human cost, choices that will actually increase suffering and political unrest. Today, all of us are witnessing the early events that could result in widespread hunger in the United States. These are only our first encounters with the growing inaccessibility of food, our most critical resource.

There is still time to substitute self-reliance and sound values for the blind following of almost blind leaders. We can still influence public policy and firmly grasp control of our own futures. It is not too late to reverse the trajectory and create a new way of life that is stronger, richer and more rewarding than the present way. There is still time to solve the problem of hunger in America and in the world . . . but there is no longer much time.

The per acre yield of all cereals peaked back in the early 1970s. Since then there has been only decline. Topsoil being lost through erosion exceeds that being formed by nature. Since the mid-1970s, a third of all U.S. cropland has suffered soil losses too great to be sustained without a gradual, but ultimately disastrous, decline in productivity.

Each day brings more news about the rising cost of food, the failure of small farms, the instability and increasing inadequacy of the Social Security system, President Reagan's budget cuts, and the shortage of energy. Every week the facts and the statistics change. The focus of the crisis frequently shifts. For that reason I felt that the lives of the people who are directly affected by these critical changes more clearly reflect the impact of where we are all headed. The experts and the statistics tell one part of the story. But the ways that the changes are weakening and damaging America are best understood by letting the men, women, and children whose lives are affected speak their thoughts. Through them the meaning and impact of the events become clear.

It is apparent that the entire country will face and have to deal with many of these issues. We can learn from those who have already confronted them. Americans can no longer smugly label the hungry as incompetent and then forget them.

I believe that the kinds of changes that are occurring in America can provide us with new opportunities, new answers, and permanent solutions based on a new awareness of our own vulnerability and a new respect for each other and for the fragile balances in nature which support all life.

Despite that, I fully expect that many people will not accept the concepts or the conclusions of this book. Often they are not pleasant. Sometimes they deal with political abuse and government-sanctioned suppression of workable solutions. Many of us would rather not deal with such concepts, but the rapid succession of crises that are currently affecting all of us clearly indicates that the most certain way to fulfill the worst prophecies is to ignore them, and to continue on our present course until it becomes irreversible.

Some people may point to a particular statistic

in this book that has changed or has been calculated differently. While I strove for accuracy, I'd like to point out that statistics themselves are constantly changing and are subject to interpretation and political manipulation. I am less concerned with the precise numbers than with the clear and undeniable fact that millions of Americans are hungry, and that millions more face substantial risk of hunger in the near future. It is also clear that if we changed our policies no one would have to be hungry. Those facts, and the reasons for them, convinced me that people needed to address these problems. I am simply a journalist who has sought out, recorded, and compiled the opinions of experts in each specific field. Beyond that I have tried to transcribe accurately the the pain, and the dignity of the rural and urban poor, and of the starving and malnourished people of America.

2   Dying Slowly

No fear can stand up to hunger, no patience can wear
it out, disgust simply does not exist where hunger is;
and as to superstition, beliefs, and what you may call
principles, they are less than chaff in a breeze.
    —Joseph Conrad, *Heart of Darkness*

An emaciated woman pulled at the edges of a torn gray sweater, her bony fingers red in the cold. She leaned heavily on the porch railing for support. Her body was still but her large bright blue eyes darted back and forth. Her head turned less quickly, and because she was so thin, the muscles and tendons of her neck stood out. She was waiting for food. As the car eased to the curb below her porch on Weld Hill Street in Boston, the woman began to come down the steps with what seemed like almost frantic gestures. She was at the door of the car as the director of the Ecumenical Social Action Committee's Senior Citizens' lunch program turned off the engine.

"How are you today?" the director asked politely, handing her the packaged lunch and starting to close the car door before the woman could respond.

"I'm very weak," the woman said quickly. The words were clipped, the voice high and nervous, with a Boston-Irish accent. Although she spoke well, as a person who was educated, there was fear in her voice and in everything else about her.

She was almost a living skeleton. Her eyes were framed by huge dark circles, but the ashen skin, stretched tightly, still revealed a small, upturned nose and finely shaped lips, which made it clear that she had once been beautiful.

"I need help. Will you come back? You must come back," she pleaded, her voice trembling.

"You know that we're very busy and we have a lot of other meals to deliver," the director answered as she turned the key in the ignition.

"I'll come back," I said as the car drove off.

I went back later that afternoon.

The woman explained to me that once she had done civil service work in City Hall, then had served with the Boston School Committee as a legal secretary.

She lost her job several years ago, and after her unemployment compensation ran out she applied for welfare. They said she could work, and she said she wants to work, but no one will hire her.

"I've had no income and I've paid no rent for many months. My landlord let me stay. He felt sorry for me because I had no money. The Friday before Christmas he gave me ten dollars. For days I had had nothing but water. I knew I needed food; I tried to go out but I was too weak to walk to the store. I felt as if I were dying. I saw the mailman and told him I thought I was starving. He brought me food and then he made some phone calls and that's when they began delivering these lunches. But I had already lost so much weight that five meals a week are not enough to keep me going.

"I just pray to God I can survive. I keep praying I can have the will to save some of my food so I can divide it up and make it last. It's hard to save because I am so hungry that I want to eat it right away. On Friday, I held over two peas from the lunch. I ate one pea on Saturday morning. Then I got into bed with the taste of food in my mouth and I waited as long as I could. Later on in the day I ate the other pea.

"Today I saved the container that the mashed potatoes were in and tonight, before bed, I'll lick the sides of the container.

"When there are bones I keep them. I know this is going to be hard for you to believe and I am almost ashamed to tell you, but these days I boil the bones till they're soft and then I eat them. Today there were no bones."

Upstairs, the old double bed was filled with neatly stacked piles of papers. The woman told me that they were mostly copies of letters she had written to the Social Security office, the Department of Public Welfare, and to local church groups and lawyers, pleading for food. Social workers from local social service agencies claimed that they had done all that they could. They said that they tried repeatedly to help her but that she had failed to qualify or had been unwilling to follow their rules, and as a result she would have to subsist on five meals a week.

I walked into the small clean kitchen and

opened the refrigerator. Except for the container with
the bit of mashed potatoes left from lunch, it was
empty. There was absolutely no food in any of the
cupboards.

"It's happening all over this city," said Dorothy
Lynch, a social worker at the Dorchester Area
Planning Action Council, a federally funded anti-
poverty program. "People are starving. For one
reason or another they don't meet all thirty-six
requirements for food stamps. They can't get welfare;
they're too old for the job market and too young for
Social Security. What can we tell them to do," she
asked angrily, "go to the hospital and get treated for
malnutrition?

"The other day I was at the welfare office. A
woman who had been waiting in line there had
passed out from lack of food. People were saying she
was drunk but I knew she wasn't. She had the
bloated belly and the look around her eyes. They took
her to the hospital and found out that she was just
malnourished from living on cat food—right here in
Dorchester."

Hunger—so acute that it made grown women in
America eat tree bark, laundry starch, and anything
else available—was meticulously documented in the
late 1960s by the Citizens' Board of Inquiry, a
twenty-five member board led by Ford Foundation
executive, Richard Boone. The board had determined
to examine government food aid programs. Soon
after its members sprang into action they were
moving into poverty pockets throughout the nation.
In the summer of 1967, its researchers reported that
babies were dying because there was no milk in their
mothers' breasts and no money with which to buy
milk. They discovered that organic brain damage,
retarded growth and learning rates, disease, with-

drawal, apathy, frustration, and violence were all part of the toll of hunger in America. They found and identified kwashiorkor and marasmus, diseases of extreme protein and calorie deficiency, thought to exist only in underdeveloped countries.

Actually, that kind of severe hunger had been brought to the committee's attention and to public attention. Three months earlier, in April 1967, after Senators Robert F. Kennedy and Joseph Clark drove along the bleak, unpaved back roads of the Mississippi Delta, stopping at shack after shack and seeing for themselves some of the starving, diseased, and retarded children of America. The men got out of their cars. They put out their hands and touched the children's swollen stomachs. They tried to talk to them but the children were too hungry, too apathetic, or too badly damaged to respond.

"I have seen bad things in West Virginia," said Robert Kennedy, badly shaken, "but I've never seen anything like this anywhere in the United States."[1]

Kennedy reported his findings and the federal government vowed to correct the situation. Senators George S. McGovern, Ernest F. Hollings, and Robert J. Dole joined the effort. In 1969 Richard Nixon called for the first White House Conference on Food, Nutrition and Health. It was presided over by Dr. Jean Mayer, of Harvard, one of the country's leading nutritionists. The conference involved deliberations by five thousand Americans; recommendations were made and many were acted upon and some people thought that the problems of hunger and malnutrition in the United States had been solved.

In 1980, when a specially appointed presidential commission on world hunger released its preliminary report, only two of the sixteen conclusions set forth dealt with hunger in America. The first stated that some segments of the American population, notably migrant workers and Native Americans, remained "vulnerable" to malnutrition. The other praised the success of the federal feeding programs and recommended "modifications to improve their availability to the poor, better mechanisms for reaching certain groups and closer monitoring of local administrative practices." There was also a general call for "prosperous nations to address their problems of hunger."

The president's commissioners were deeply committed to assuring that people in America who were poor did not need to be hungry as well, but it also believed that the government had reduced the problem of hunger so substantially that no intensive attention was required.

A 1980 report by the Field Foundation, a courageous organization funded by the Marshall Field Department Store family and especially concerned with the poor, had come to the same conclusion. A group of physicians had returned to some of the poverty areas that had been visited in the 1960s. The physicians found that those areas that were targets of federal aid had improved greatly; indeed many of them had. And yet, in my own seven year investigation, I found that many other areas had not improved.

In August 1979, more than twelve years after Robert Kennedy's report to the government, I retraced some of his steps. I flew to Memphis, Tennessee, and drove a hundred miles south on Highway 61. I stopped in Mound Bayou, Mississippi, the oldest all-black town in America, and spent three days at the federally funded Delta Community Health Center.

"Whole families come here malnourished,"

Caroline Broussard, a young, articulate black physician, who trained at Tulane University and Kansas University Medical School, told me. "But what's worse is that we know that for every hungry child or adult we see here in this clinic there are twenty or thirty others in the area we are *not* getting to. It's a mess. I've been here for three years. The War on Poverty was well-intentioned but they didn't take the time to really understand or meet the needs of the people."

"These people are struggling day to day," she said. "I really don't know how they do it. How they survive. They live in shacks, little old shacks, right here in Mound Bayou. The water is so filthy; it is brown and the people drink it every day because they don't have anything else. I shouldn't be seeing people in the United States using the yard for a bathroom, and washing with rainwater. You have to understand I am talking about people living in places not fit for a dog to live and going without food."

"First, and before everything, these people are hungry. How do you tell them they have to love their children better if they are hungry? They come to this setting and I ask them to do things the way middle-class people would. But how can they if they are hungry?"

I knew exactly what she was talking about. I had seen hunger bordering on starvation in cities all across America, yet many well-intentioned public officials had laughed at me when I asked them if they thought there was hunger in their city. As I sat there with Dr. Broussard, I remembered the disbelief and then the shock of Alan Halpern, my first editor, when I came back to his office and told him about Anna Jones.

Anna and her nine children lived in a boarded-up section of North Philadelphia near Fifteenth Street and Susquehanna Avenue. Paint fell from the walls of tenement buildings, broken windows went unreplaced, and even the shattered glass seemed never to be picked up. Men sat around on empty orange crates and graffiti covered almost everything. It was as if, having learned how to write, the kids were at a loss for something to say and a place to say it. On one building in the Joneses' neighborhood someone had written "cat chow" and "horsemeat" larger than the four-letter obscenities.

These were the streets the Jones kids played in and walked through when they went to school. But when I found them, the children had been going to school less and less. Inside the school's administrative office there was a steadily growing fear that these children were in danger of starving to death. The school officials were still a little afraid to say anything definitive, afraid of making a mistake. But one nurse involved with the case admitted that the kids were getting worse. After that, the school counselor wrote a letter to the Department of Welfare explaining that a caseworker found the house unfit for human habitation and that on a recent visit to the house the children were found eating a box of laundry starch.

As we stood shivering in front of Mrs. Jones's house, the counselor explained that there were plenty of other cases like this in Philadelphia—some were worse. In the dark living room Mrs. Jones sat huddled in a bathrobe, on the only piece of furniture in the house, a torn green couch, partially covered by a dirty sheet. A plastic trash bag covered one of the broken windows but the wind tore through the others, past the living room into the empty kitchen, and down the rubbish strewn, mouse-infested stairway to the cellar.

"Mrs. Jones, do you have any food in the house?" the counselor had asked.

"Yes, I have food."

We looked in the refrigerator. The only thing there was some kind of orange liquid that had spilled and hardened along the bottom shelf and a single can of solidified fat. The kitchen cabinet hadn't one item of food. A pot sat on the hot plate with an old tea bag floating in its cold water.

The children came downstairs dressed in the school outfits given to them by the Department of Welfare at the beginning of the year. These were still quite new looking, perhaps because the children had attended school so little. They came in silently and lined up, trembling without coats, behind the couch. Their hands were numb with cold, but they stood there, like little Spartans in their mother's army, determined to be loyal to her.

"Are you cold?" I asked.

"No," said a nine-year-old girl, speaking for the group.

"Are you hungry?"

"No."

"When did you last eat?"

"We're not hungry," she said deliberately.

"Does your mother have food?"

"Yes," she said, "she does."

It was as if those kids had memorized a liturgy before their mother brought them down from the bedroom, where they slept on torn, filthy mattresses without sheets or blankets or pillows. Or perhaps hunger and cold had numbed them almost beyond feeling. The four-year-old boy didn't move. He simply stared off into space and the seventeen-month-old infant just sat there drinking water from a bottle. I was told she had never uttered a word.

Before I left I saw something in the eyes of one of the children. A desire to communicate—something. He was Paul, a boy of eight, but his physical growth had already been retarded by about three years. I bent down, "Would you like to come back to school with us?" I asked. "It's warm at school and there are lunches."

He didn't say anything. He didn't have to. He just looked at me hard, for a long serious moment, then slowly he lifted his hand and gently, tentatively, touched my cold fingers with his. I smiled. His large brown eyes filled with tears. Then he nodded.

Now, sitting with Dr. Broussard in Mound Bayou, Mississippi, I tried to reassure her that I did understand, at least a little, about the pain of the poor and the hungry, and I hoped I understood a little about how they managed to survive somehow, against overwhelming odds, and even to defend and protect each other and find some genuine joys despite all the suffering. I wanted to convince her that the general lack of understanding stemmed from the fact that most people knew so little about hunger in this country.

She agreed with me and I think was beginning to trust me. We went on trying to find answers. "If we brought food in and patched up the roof and cleaned up the house, maybe we could start teaching these people about other things," she reasoned out loud. "But until then the War on Poverty is not going to work."

Dr. Broussard wanted to teach the poor how to have a chance at life. Not just a chance at survival. She wanted to do more than provide a clinic where the malnourished could be treated for hunger-related illnesses. When I asked her if food stamps and WIC (the Women, Infants and Children program), which provides a supplementary feeding program for mothers and young children, were accomplishing some of these things, she reprimanded me gently and then explained: "Most of the families who get food stamps don't know how to buy food. They buy junk at high prices and use a month's allotment in two weeks. You have to understand that these people are way below poverty level, way below. As for WIC," she continued, wanting me to know the way it "really" was, "think of it this way. You have twelve people living in a shack and you give the mother and infant a small supply of milk, eggs, and cheese. It should be clear to you that the whole family's going to devour that food. I mean the entire family. Does the government really think they have taken care of the hunger problem here? Well, I'm sorry, it's just not that way.

"We have nutrition profiles of these families," she continued. "We have extreme malnutrition. So extreme that the children don't grow normally. I just discharged a child today. She's a year old and she looks like she is eight months old. Her psychomotor development is that of an eight-month-old. We can't help her because we simply don't have the facilities to follow a child like that."

It starts with retarded physical development, but often the children in Mississippi get worse, not better. Even now, some end up with kwashiorkor, a protein-deficiency disease so severe that despite the fact that it was identified in the United States most people mistakenly think it was wiped out and that it now exists only in the underdeveloped countries. Kwashiorkor, which has a death rate of up to 80 percent, is characterized by hair turning dry and orange and swelling of the legs and belly.

44

Dr. Broussard told me that she had recently treated a baby with kwashiorkor and found that it wasn't caused by neglect on the part of the mother. She gave her baby daughter milk when she had it, when she could get it. But like so many others, she lived from day to day, from hand to mouth, with no plumbing, just an outhouse and rainwater collected in pots and little tubs. She was malnourished herself. The next-door neighbor brought her and the baby in. When the social services people went out to her house and looked in the cabinets, they found that there was no food in the house. The hospital kept that baby for four weeks. When she improved, they gave the mother food and found that she was actually a very good parent.

"We've heard a lot of rumors here," Dr. Broussard said, expressing her impatience very openly. "Everybody wants to say there is no poverty, no hunger in the United States, that if a child is hungry it's the mother's fault. They are crazy. There is a lot of politics in poverty and in starvation. I went to Washington and Califano's [Joseph A. Califano, Jr., former secretary of the then Department of Health, Education, and Welfare (HEW)] undersecretary patted me on the shoulder and said, 'We know you guys are doing a real fine job.' How does he know we are doing a real fine job? *He* has never been here. *He* has never seen people starving and dying. These people are barely living—*just* barely. When I ask them if they know that they don't have to live like this, they look at me and say, 'No, ma'am, I didn't.' They actually think that they have to be starving and diseased."

Disease is accepted as commonplace in the lives of these people, second only to hunger. Marasmus, for example, has been identified in Mound Bayou.

Characterized by severe tissue wasting from deficiency of both calories and protein, it can certainly result from what many of these people live on. "We can't document it," Dr. Broussard said. "We can't prove what we're saying. We don't have the facilities to document it and that makes it easy for others to close their eyes and pretend that hunger in America doesn't exist."

Actually, no one in this country has documented the effects of hunger on a large scale. No significant technical study of hunger in America has ever been made. During the antihunger efforts in the late 1960s, Congress did order a scientific investigation of hunger and malnutrition. A resulting ten-state survey found that nutritional inadequacies had led to the mental and physical stunting of many poor American children. That study also identified cases of kwashiorkor and marasmus. But funding for the investigation was unexpectedly cut off. Many of its proponents believed that the funding had been stopped because admission by HEW of serious malnutrition in the United States was embarrassing and politically unacceptable.

Dr. Arnold Shaeffer, the physician who conducted the ten-state study, quietly told me, "We now know beyond any doubt that a mother's malnourishment could produce an infant who is retarded in its ability to grow. We also fear that there may be reduction in the total number of brain cells—and that these children never catch up. This is a permanent retardation. By age one and a half, eighty percent of the total brain cell number and size has been reached. By age four, brain-cell development is ninety-four to ninety-seven percent complete. So the earlier the insult the greater the chance of brain damage. This should alert us. This should not

46

happen in the United States. It behooves us to use every procedure possible to make certain we eradicate this situation of risk."

Instead, the study was buried and Americans were never told about it or about the extent of hunger in the United States or the forms it took. Nor were Americans ever told what it would mean if the United States food supply or food distribution network was temporarily cut off or sharply reduced.

The only carefully documented scientific account of hunger and starvation that I've encountered was made by a group of physicians who were condemned to die from the conditions they were studying. That investigation was made in 1940 in the Warsaw Ghetto. The Nazis had sealed several hundred thousand Jews off from the rest of the world. Their purpose was mass extermination through mass starvation.

In the midst of the resulting chaos, hunger, pain, and disease, an extraordinary group of physicians determined to record the clinical, metabolic, and pathologic consequences of starvation. They smuggled research equipment into the ghetto and secretly recorded their findings. Then, when they knew that their own time had run out and that the deportation and death of those left alive were about to begin, they gave their unfinished manuscript to the director of the Department of Medicine at Warsaw University. He in turn buried it for safe-keeping.

In addition to being an extraordinary document and a tribute to the fact that the human spirit and the drive to understand can sometimes stretch beyond all imaginable boundaries, the findings of these physicians, recently translated from the Polish, provide Americans with the most detailed scientific account of the effects that hunger and starvation have had. The study prepares us Americans for what we can expect if our own food supply or distribution systems fail. It also explains much of what is already happening to the chronically hungry people living in Mississippi and elsewhere in the United States.

In the Warsaw Ghetto the inhabitants were officially limited to 800 calories a day. The diet consisted of less than five percent fat, fifteen percent vegetable protein, and more than eighty percent carbohydrate. Some got fewer than the allotted 800 calories, while others managed to eat a little more with food smuggled into the ghetto.

With this pattern of food supply, the physicians found that the first symptoms of malnutrition, "hunger disease," as the secret report called it, were of thirst, rapid weight loss, and a constant craving for food. With prolonged hunger, these symptoms diminished and the patients experienced general weakness and an inability to sustain even the smallest physical effort. They became unwilling to work and remained in bed all day, covered because they always felt cold, especially in the nose and extremities. They became apathetic and depressed and lacked initiative. "They do not remember their hunger," one physician wrote, "but when shown bread, meat, or sweets, they become very aggressive, grab the food and devour it at once, even though they may be beaten for it and have no strength to run away."

Toward the end of hunger disease, the only complaint is complete exhaustion. Very often edema appears and for this reason hunger disease has also been called edema disease. Edema usually appears first on the face, followed by swelling of the feet and legs, especially in people who walk or stand a great deal. In the early stages the edema disappears during bed rest. In the late stages edema affects the whole body. At first, large urinary output and constant thirst are dominant, but these symptoms disappear in the later stages of hunger. Then there are complaints of aches and pains in the ribs, sternum, pelvis, and the lower extremities, and of nervousness and anxiety, but few psychic abnormalities. Women miss their menstrual periods and are sterile. Men are impotent. And the few children who are born die within a few weeks.[1] The physicians also found that when tissue started to disappear, the faces of hungry people looked younger for a short time then later, in the second and third stages of hunger, men, and especially women, looked very old. "Boys and girls from blooming roses change into withered old people." The passage from life to death is slow and gradual, like death from physiological old age. There is nothing violent. No dyspnea, no pain, no obvious change in breathing or circulation. Vital functions subside simultaneously. Pulse rate and respiratory rate are slower and it becomes more and more difficult to reach the patient's sense of awareness, until life is gone. People who starve to death often fall asleep in bed or on the street and are dead in the morning.

Dr. Israel Milejkowski, the physician who led the study in the Warsaw Ghetto, left this message for the survivors: ". . . I tell you, my beloved colleagues and companions in misery. You are a part of all of us. Slavery, hunger, deportation, those death figures in our ghetto were also your legacy. And you by your work could give the henchman the answer *'non omnis moriar,'* 'I shall not wholly die.' "[2]

For three days I sat in the clinic in Mound Bayou, Mississippi, watching another group who were hungry and diseased file through. Their ancestors had also once been prisoners and slaves. I was struck by the commonality of the suffering that was shared by the hungry everywhere, how needlessly cruel their lives were, and how we are all ultimately diminished by allowing such conditions to persist.

Many of these people still thought of themselves as slaves. They were always ready for the next punishment, the next insult, the next piece of bad news. Most expected to be hungry and sick a lot of the time, and many still referred to the white plantation owners, whose land they lived on, as the master.

Mary Hampton, who now works in the clinic as a nurse's aide, grew up picking cotton on a plantation. She survived the system but she clearly remembers the victimization. "On the plantation, your food, your money, everything you got you had to get from the master," she told me. "One time my daddy picked twenty-six bales of cotton. It took him from August to December. After all that work was done the master paid him four dollars and some cents, then, right after he gave the money to him, the master told my daddy that he wasn't allowed to spend it because he owed it right back again for the cotton seed. Later when Daddy sold his cotton the master told him the money he got would just barely pay back his debt. The master called that 'sharecropping.' But what it really meant was when you got through with all your work you wouldn't get nothing and if you told anyone or complained you'd come up killed on the river."

Since those days of her childhood Mary Hampton's own life had changed considerably. "Personally I'm doing a hundred percent better than I was and I like it. But these other folks that we take care of here are still living the way I did as a child. They ain't got no food to eat or no money to get it, and, honey, I tell you even the roof on their heads don't count cause you have to stuff rags in it to keep the rain out."

Our conversation was interrupted when Dr. Walter Gough, the clinic's dedicated young director, came into the examining room carrying an infant. "This is Donald," he said, "he's two months old today. His hemoglobin and hematocrit are now way below the minimum for his age. He's been losing weight. He's lost a lot of water. His skin has lost its elasticity. Notice how, if we pull it up, it just stays there. His problem is caused by lack of adequate nutrition. We'll have to admit him to the hospital and try to make him well."

Next came Bernetta, age six months. Bernetta had diarrhea for two weeks. The stools were green. Her body and head were covered with sores. There was pus in her ears and her hemoglobin was way below normal. Bernetta was on a high-starch diet. She, too, was suffering from a lack of adequate nutrition.

Before Bernetta was off the examining table the nurse entered carrying another infant and saying the hemoglobin on this one was so low that if it wasn't raised quickly there would be brain damage. Turning to me, she added that she had seen more malnutrition, hunger, and anemia here in three weeks than she'd seen before in her entire life.

They filed through like that all day. Eileen, a beautiful, frail, badly undernourished child of ten, was the last patient. She sat on the edge of the examining table wide-eyed and trembling, in her filthy white-and-red polka-dot dress. Somehow she had gotten some nail polish and had worked hard at making her hands, which she kept very clean, look pretty. She smiled tentatively at me, and then more boldly she told me she liked my shoes. After she left, Dr. Gough explained that Eileen was suffering from a goiter caused by a lack of iodine in her diet. "You know," he said, shaking his head sadly, "unbelievable as it is, many of these families have it rougher now than they did twenty years ago."

Wanting to help me understand the almost incomprehensible suffering, he explained that the machines had gotten rid of the cotton pickers and that these people had traded poverty with work for poverty without work. Some of the plantation owners had let them stay on. But since they no longer needed them they had stopped caring about what kind of shape they were in. They allowed them to remain on the plantation only because the U.S. Internal Revenue Service considered them the landowners' dependents, as long as they got no federal aid. If they went on welfare or accepted food coupons they could no longer be written off by the owners as tax deductions. What that really meant was that if they applied for help they would lose their homes. As a result, they got neither welfare, food stamps, nor work.

"We did a study in 1965," Dr. Gough added, "and found that ninety-five percent of the blacks in this four-county area made less than nine hundred dollars a year. What little we can do for them here becomes less each year. Our funds are constantly being cut. This started out as an eight-million-dollar program in 1969, serving two hundred thousand people in a four-county area, and even that was only six percent of those living below the poverty level. If a larger number came to us we simply wouldn't be able to serve them."

"But, Doctor," I said, "what about the other ninety-four percent? What happens to the ninety-four percent that you never see?"

He shrugged. "They survive the best they can," and then he shook his head sadly and his voice trailed off, *"or else they die."*

3 Middle-Class and Hungry

Nothing more overwhelms the human spirit, or mocks our values and our dreams, than the desperate struggle for sustenance.
—Dr. Henry Kissinger
World Food Conference
Rome, November 1974

Hunger is more difficult to identify in the big cities than it is in rural areas like Mound Bayou, Mississippi, but usually there is no less of it. Proportionately there is probably more. But in the cities the hungry tend to remain hidden or lost in the crowds, especially the elderly who had always been part of the working middle class. For them, hunger and poverty are new and humiliating. The shame, the fear, and the physical weakness hunger creates in them frequently make them withdraw more. Often they are afraid to seek help or venture out until they are near collapse.

No one seemed to know, for example, that Raymond Zagone was living alone without food in his apartment in an old building in uptown Chicago until the building manager found him sprawled on the landing. Only then did he tell her that it had been four days since he'd had any food; only then did he ask her to help. She, in turn, contacted the Senior Centers of Metropolitan Chicago and they began delivering the usual package. Five meals a week.

It was suppertime on a Thursday when I arrived to visit Mr. Zagone. I climbed the three flights of stairs and knocked. In the light from the hallway, I saw a small, very thin old man. His skin hung loosely as he stood in the doorway, stark-naked and trembling. He peered up at me, confused. His small, almond-shaped eyes were dark with questioning.

"I have come to talk to you about food," I said.

"Yes, lady," Raymond Zagone responded tentatively, "come in."

I stepped inside, leaving the door to the hall open because it was dark in the room. Then he turned on the light, sat down, and covered himself with a dirty blanket. Roaches crawled across my feet. I tried to brush them off each foot with the opposite shoe. He was watching me, waiting.

"Do you have any food in the house?" I asked, wanting not to seem uncomfortable, forcing myself to go on with the interview.

"No, ma'am, I don't," he answered quietly.

Then, still wrapped in the blanket, he led me into the tiny kitchen and opened the refrigerator. There was one moldy bone on the bottom shelf.

"I understand that you now get five lunches a week from the Senior Centers of Metropolitan

Chicago," I said. "Is it enough?"

"Oh, I don't know."

"What about the weekends?" I asked, knowing that no food was brought to him on Saturdays or Sundays. "Do you eat anything from Friday to Monday?"

"No, lady, I don't. Sometimes I get very hungry," he responded, shaking his head. "But what can I do? Whatever happens to me, I just have to take it.

"A lady came around two months ago," he confided. "She asked if she could clean my apartment. I was very happy. I said yes, thank you, but she didn't clean, she just pretended, you know, to dust a little while she looked around, then she said she'd be right back and left. I didn't know it till later but she robbed me. She took all of my money."

Since then Zagone's small monthly Social Security check has been carefully hidden. Suddenly, for some reason, he decided to trust me. He reached under the mattress and took out an unopened envelope from the Social Security Administration and said proudly, "I have money again."

"Mr. Zagone," I ventured, feeling that we were friends now, "don't these roaches bother you?"

"Yes, they do, they bother me very much. They crawl over me when I sleep. They wake me up, and in the bed something bites me."

"Did anyone ever spray the place to get rid of some of these bugs?"

"No," he said thoughtfully, shaking his head, "I wish they do."

Then he told me about life years earlier in Mexico, about his two sisters and one brother back in Torreón, who are dead now. "I fought in the Mexican Revolution in 1910," he said, his eyes shining, his few yellow teeth exposed by the smile. "I drove a taxi

56

when I came to this country. I made a good living. I had many friends. I spoke to many people. But now," dropping his head sadly, he said, with a resignation that almost made him sound childlike, "I don't have anything or anybody. You know," he continued, as if he had been brought back many years, "I do like to have friends very much. They are good to me, and I am good to them, but tell me where can I find one? I am afraid to go outside and yet I am alone and I am lonely. Without a friend, I am nobody."

Later, when I told him it was time for me to go, he kissed my hand and held onto my arm for a long time. Then, at his request, I turned out the light. When I closed the door, he was sitting on the bed, still naked under his ragged blanket, staring off into the darkness, tapping his fingers on his knee and trembling quietly.

I began this book with the premise that there was a connection between the people I found starving in 1974 and the social and moral values that would cause hunger to increase in the coming years.

The roots of that connection go back much further than the 1970s. They are linked to an attitude or to many attitudes that grew with American affluence. Since the end of the Depression, America had experienced a rising wave of prosperity. With seemingly endless resources and an increasing number of options, life for the majority became easier but also more careless. Everything moved so quickly that many people lost a foothold in the old stable values, the traditional ways of doing things, or deciding what needed to be done. As the scale of life and what seemed to be opportunity increased, many Americans grew indifferent to the moral systems and the people they had once thought important. The main concern became personal fulfillment. This was the "me" generation, the "now" decade.

Even the goals of the moment became more transitory. Advanced technology made so much disposable that it became simpler and cheaper to abandon things than to preserve them. Mass media and jet planes bombarded Americans with possibilities that seemed as endless as our resources.

It didn't seem to matter. In fact, most middle-class people barely knew that thirty million Americans lived below the poverty line or that many of our senior citizens were dismally poor; people were so involved in understanding themselves and fully exploiting the moment that they failed to understand what was really in their interest. As the values and connections between people changed, ironically those who stood to lose most from the changes were the people who had helped to create them: the people who had built the country's prosperity—the elderly.

They simply slipped out of the public's experience and consciousness. Despite the richness of American technology and the size and complexity of the American bureaucracy, we had shown ourselves to be poor in spirit and deficient in love. We had become increasingly isolated from contact with the aged. They were where they had always been, but we were no longer there with them.

They had worked in our hospitals and banks and factories, they had driven our taxis, they had built our railroads, and they had entertained in our theaters and nightclubs. More than any other group the elderly had become victims of the society they helped to shape. When resources ran short and inflation was rampant, millions were left totally dependent on programs that had never been intended as more than supplements. Most tried against almost impossible odds to maintain independent lives. But, in 1980 the average monthly income of a person over sixty-five who had put money into the Social Security system for thirty or more years was only $289 a month or $3468 a year.

I asked a social service outreach worker at the Albert Einstein Medical Center in Philadelphia about her work with the elderly and heard this. "It is very depressing to sit with these people and say I know it's rough, I know you're starving, but I have no answers. I am talking about people who get one hundred and fifty-five dollars a month and say to themselves, let's see, how can I do it, how can I survive? I have the gas, the fuel, the electric, the medicine. . . . If they are lucky, they have fifteen dollars a month in food stamps. What can you eat with fifteen dollars? That's fifty cents a day, or less than seventeen cents a meal. I don't know how much worse it can be. If you were thirty or thirty-five perhaps you could find an alternative means of living, but when you are seventy, seventy-five, eighty years old, trying to live on this kind of income is impossible. When you open their cupboards you see an egg, two eggs, an onion, they are living from day to day.

"Many people think when you are a senior citizen you get a lot of extras like hot, home-delivered meals," she continued angrily, "but when you actually try to get them you are told that there are three hundred and seventy-six people ahead of you. You have to wait until they die. Some of these people can't get to the stores, or if they get there, they can't afford the food, or else their expenses are so high that they can't afford the dental care. If they get the teeth they can't afford the meat. It's a catch-22 with the elderly getting it from all sides."

I also learned that afternoon that Medicare

covers some things, but not others. If a person goes to a doctor and is told that he or she needs drugs, which cost four or five dollars, that person may be forced to choose between the medicine and food.

If they are given an increase in Social Security someone is sent out to reevaluate them, and the raise is deducted from their food stamps.

"When we have a social function at the hospital where I work, we serve food," the director of social services explained, "and the elderly people come with shopping bags. First, they pile their plates with food, then they wrap it up and put it away. They take anything that's not nailed down. Most of it is deprivation, not a lack of manners. It's a need that's overwhelming. They see a tray of cheese and think, Oh, my God, when was the last time I had cheese? It's survival, that's what it is. I believe that many of these people are suffering from varying stages of malnutrition. They are starving slowly while trying, on a day-to-day basis, to survive...."

This is South Philadelphia—a microcosm of America, a place where people have gone to work, raised children, and then retired. Their daughters are our secretaries, clerks, and teachers. Their sons are our policemen, longshoremen, bankers, doctors, and lawyers. Economically these retired people once represented America's middle class. Yet in this typical urban neighborhood with its tap dance school, businessmen's association, American Cancer Society chapter, and local fire station, a two-year survey conducted by the Albert Einstein Medical Center's Social Service Division concluded that "very few if any of the elderly were without need."

These are men and women who have worked all their lives. These are our uncles, our aunts, our grandparents, our mothers, and our fathers. They live in a world of old newspaper clippings, pictures, and photographs of relatives who never visit.

To say that the Social Security they receive is not enough is an understatement. To say that the much touted 14 percent increase in July 1980 raised the average recipient's yearly payments up to $3,960 still doesn't express it. More painful even than their poverty is their awareness that they have been left behind to die. Even if Social Security were enough to allow these people to eat the food that they needed and enough to allow them to pay their bills, it would still be inadequate. Because meeting only the survival needs of people and ignoring their psychological needs is inadequate.

Some of the men and women I spoke to accepted their situations with quiet dignity. Some denied it with courageous cheerfulness; others were overwhelmed by fear and compensated in whatever ways they could.

For Fay Grabel, who had grown up Fay Cohen, the result was a strange new alliance. Fay graduated from high school, attended Strayers Business College, and worked in Lit Brothers department store and as a bank teller before becoming a secretary. For her day she was an independent woman. She had not married Sol Grabel until she was in her late twenties. Even then, when her child was in school she continued to work as a secretary and helped Sol in their grocery store early in the morning and after five. "I loved to work," she told me. "I had so much energy that when I came home I'd run straight out again and I'd make the deliveries for Sol." Slowly everything changed. Sol had a heart attack and died. Her son grew up and moved to New Jersey, had a bad first marriage, a bad second marriage, and dropped out of sight. Fay herself grew old and frail.

"That's my grandson," she told me, pointing to the picture on the wall. "That's the boy I'm leaving my house to in my will. He's a nice boy. That's my grandson's mother and over there is my son."

"Do you ever see them?" I asked.

"Well, no, not exactly, but I think about them," she said, embarrassed. "What happened is they moved far away across the bridge to Maplewood, New Jersey," and then trying to forget, she changed the subject. "Luckily I have Mary."

I had heard about Mary from some of the social workers at Albert Einstein. No one knew exactly what was wrong with her. One said she had been brain-damaged by syphilis, another thought she was a paranoid schizophrenic because she was often seen wandering the streets alone talking out loud to herself for hours at a time about the people who were trying to kill her and steal her money.

I had one long talk with her which began logically enough but rapidly deteriorated. On that day Mary spoke of Fay.

"She had plenty trouble," Mary had explained, "she has these kidneys, then she has this terrible trouble with walking, it could be even cancer but we do know she has sugar. She has a lot of friends hither and yon and so forth. She just can't find them so she cries and worries and wants. I can't stay with her for long. I do everything to try to make her understand I have to go back to Washington, you see, child, the president of the United States himself didn't know that I was the owner of thousands of different things but then the whole world told him and the band started playing and the politicians they all knew it was me. The president began to send me money but it got took through the mail. When I was in Washington they had the parade for me. I thought that was sweet. But they don't want me to fly my planes. My own planes. They try every way to tell me I'm not the owner. They hates me because I am the owner. They try to kill me because I am part of this colored generation."

Everyone agreed they were an odd couple. The tiny, frail, old Jewish lady who could barely walk or see and who had not left her house since the day her husband died nine years before, and the deranged, homeless black woman who had been camping out in an abandoned house for at least two years, with no gas, no electricity, no nothing. It was a friendship formed of mutual need. Fay needed someone to shop for her, take care of her, and provide her with food. Mary needed a home and perhaps someone to care for and be needed by. Somehow those needs had transcended all of the others. Fay and Mary found a way to communicate with each other. It wasn't even awkward.

"She's so mixed up in so many things," Fay admits. "She lives in an imaginary world, but when it comes to doing for me she's not mixed up at all," Fay told me. "She takes care of my medicine, wonderful. She goes to the store for me, she cooks food for me. She's kind, she's like a mother to me. Honestly, I have never felt that much love and devotion in my whole life. You should see how she covers me up at night and looks after me. I have grown to love her. Before she came here she laid on the floor to sleep. She was starving. She's demented but she's kind. I only worry that she will go away and there will be no one to take care of me. I think about it day and night. What will I do if she goes to Washington like she says, and I am left alone? How will I live? How will I shop? How will I eat? I suffer from a condition called Fear. Fear is a terrible thing.

If I knew Mary would stay with me I would not be afraid, but I am constantly worried."

Despite her fear, Fay is one of the luckier people. At least for the moment she has Mary and a few thousand dollars left from her husband. She's made her adjustment.

For Theresa Scolnick, who lives down the street, life is worse. There are no children, no relatives, no Mary, and no money except for Social Security.

Theresa's concern goes beyond her own situation. She's worried about America and she feels compelled to talk about it. "I think that Jimmy Carter tried to be a good president," she tells me, "but I don't think he or the others in Washington really understood what was going on or how to control it. The price of food keeps going up and up and nobody is stopping it. Everybody feels it. It's so bad that even the rich people feel it now. When I lay down at night everything comes over me. Not just what I'm going through but this feeling I have that the world will never be the same. People were so different when I was young. They used to care about each other. They used to be so kind. These days I can't get my neighbor to drive me to the store even if I offer to pay him. Maybe it's lucky that he says no because Lord knows I can't afford to pay him much."

I looked around at the once beautiful sitting room with its two matching fireplaces and cut-glass chandelier made for five bulbs—only one bulb was being used. She read my thoughts. "I try to keep the cost of electricity down. For that matter I try to keep the cost of everything down so that I can stay here and not lose my house. For thirty years I've had this house. You can see that this was a beautiful house once, but now I can't afford to keep it up or to repair it or even light it. It's been getting worse and worse ever since my husband died. You know," she went on, being drawn back into the past, "I always wanted to die before he died. On the twenty-fifth of March, one day after my birthday, I had gone to the store and was waiting for the bus. All of a sudden, at Eighth and Market surrounded by people, I had an over-whelming feeling—that I was in the world all alone. I felt cold and I felt dark, I mean dark inside, and I stood there and I thought, my God, what's wrong with me? When I got home the police were there waiting. They told me my husband had just died. We had been married for fifty years."

These days Theresa Scolnick worries about more inflation. She doesn't know how much longer she can make the money last. When she can she buys a ton of coal for eighty dollars. Her Blue Shield and Blue Cross are forty-five dollars every other month. By the time she pays those bills and her electricity and telephone, there is almost nothing left for food. "Meat is real high," she tells me; "when I can, I buy something that looks like veal but it's not. I really don't know what it is. I buy it in four slices and then I wrap each slice separately and freeze it and try to eat it slowly. I buy oxtail; you can cook oxtail with soup or stew. I used to love shrimp and codfish. I can't buy that. Sometimes I get a piece of lamb from the neck. I buy chicken wings. I go to the Acme supermarket and wait for the cheapest meat or the food that's sometimes reduced at the end of the day. I take what's left. I'm doing without a lot of things. I eat mostly soup—but these days you can't cook a decent soup. I used to get the shin meat; today I can't get that either. I tell you, you can't eat much now. I know it's not just me. Sometimes I watch when other elderly people come into the supermarket and I see they just stand there looking around like they are hungry and lost.

"One day about a year ago I said, oh, the hell with it. The hell with everything. I went in to the butcher, and I said I'll take that large chicken, I didn't even ask how much it was. The chicken cost four ninety-eight and I bought it. It had been years since I had had chicken like that."

"Do you remember the last time you had steak?" I asked.

She laughed and waved her hand. "Steak? You can't be very serious. I don't even look in that department. Once a month I go to McDonald's for lunch. That ground meat is the closest I ever get to steak. Since you've asked me I'm going to tell you the truth. It's very, very tough."

Theresa Scolnick is one of millions of American widows who has worked all her life, receives Social Security, and still lives *below* the poverty line. A report issued by the Advisory Council on Social Security, submitted to the Congress for 1980, stated that about one out of every three aged widows was living in poverty even if they received Social Security. Benefits for elderly women who have never been married are even lower than the benefits for widows.

No one knows how many of these women are hungry or how many are dying alone after malnutrition has weakened their bodies, allowing the onset of other diseases.

But we do know that most of the women who worked long and hard for wages were usually locked into traditional female occupations. Their salaries were meager even then and their Social Security benefits which are based on the recipient's earning level are now very low. For many, survival without outside help is nearly impossible.

One unmarried woman I met at a hot-lunch site in the Rogers Park area of Chicago, where hot lunches were being served, was a very thin little lady, dressed in yellow, with short, straight white hair and an aluminum walker. Sitting off by herself at the end of a table, she put a piece of meat into her mouth but she did not chew it. She simply kept it there for a minute, then, thinking herself unnoticed, she took the meat out of her mouth and placed it in a small paper cup. Repeating the process several times, she added more meat and pieces of potato to the cup, and then she slipped the cup and its contents, as well as the plastic knife and fork, into a small orange shopping bag with artificial flowers neatly attached to the handle.

When the director came to clear her plate, the woman smiled and quietly nodded and asked for more. This time she swallowed the food. Then she rose on her toothpick legs and began to struggle up the five steps that led from the dining room. She had devised a method to get both lunch and dinner. She had devised a method to get around the city's rule that no food could be removed from the table and taken home. A method to stay alive.

"Most of us here are alone," she explained later. "In that respect I am like the others, only I had cataracts on both my eyes. I don't see well enough to cook and since I was never married my Social Security check is lower so I don't have enough money to buy food. For those reasons I need the lunches. Sometimes I walk all the way here, and they tell me the place is full.

"I have been an orphan all my life; I grew up in nine institutions. I was never really trained for much. Someone took me into the printing trade, and I typed. Now I live on Social Security. It's about a hundred and sixty dollars a month, and my rent is a hundred and forty, so you can see where that leaves me. Once in a while, if I have a little money, I stop at the store near the K-Mart under the El. They sell cheese when the date is past, and it's at least a third cheaper. Whenever I can, I buy cheese."

The Social Security Administration recently recommended a change in policy. If it were implemented it would ensure that any person who had worked for thirty years or more with earnings equal to the minimum wage at the time would receive benefits at age sixty-five at least "equal to the poverty level."[3]

They also recommended that total benefits for all recipients gradually be brought "up" to the poverty level through the combined effects of Social Security and Supplemental Security Income.

The Social Security Administration means well, but the proposed increases are not likely to be implemented because in 1980, even without the increases, Social Security payments to beneficiaries exceeded income from payroll deductions of work-force salaries by $2.3 billion.

In fact, Social Security faces an imminent crisis in the inevitable depletion of its biggest source of money, the Federal Old-Age and Survivors Insurance Trust Fund. That is the fund which pays monthly checks to retired people. Without new financing legislation the old-age fund will be unable to pay its benefits by late 1981 or early 1982. Even with new legislation, inflation, declining gross national product, and unemployment might still deplete the entire system.

Part of the problem is that when an employer deducts Social Security taxes from a paycheck, that money, along with the employer's "contribution," goes into a general fund, which is used for current government expenses of all kinds. Then, when it is time to pay monthly benefits to the elderly, the U.S. Treasury issues the checks and prints money to cover it. All of the money being paid is newly created at the time of payment. Printing money to cover these costs creates enormous inflation, which the government tries to counteract by taking still more money out of workers' paychecks. Because it is the largest single obligation of government, the Social Security system's inflation-creating policies may cause the nation to go bankrupt before it goes broke itself.[4]

According to a recent federal statement of liabilities issued by the Treasury Department, the Social Security system had approximately $4 trillion in unfunded obligations. That means it will have to pay out $4 trillion more in benefits to those who are presently covered by the system than it will collect in wages. That's roughly equal to 75 percent of everything that everyone in America owns.[5] This is the plan that thirty-five million people are depending on for survival. Even if it keeps on going, and the proposed increases are instituted, Social Security would only allow the majority of its recipients a poverty level income after a lifetime of work.

The elderly banked on a system that doesn't work. In many cases they also counted on the love, respect, and care of family and friends who have vanished, or are too busy with the concerns, struggles, and victories of the moment even to establish contact.

One woman I met in Chicago was so alone that she had to pay a neighbor to lift her in and out of her wheelchair. Her husband was dead, her children were grown and gone. If her wheelchair got stuck, she just had to stay wherever she was until the neighbor came. Sometimes that would take a day or two.

I knocked on the door of her small white frame

house on Chicago's North Side and then opened it. Inside, Evelyn Tomlin, a tiny, white-haired woman with soft pale skin, was expecting me. She sat huddled in her wheelchair. Her small body was paralyzed by strokes and it sloped to one side. Her hands hung listlessly, but she smiled and her blue eyes twinkled with pleasure when she saw me.

It was a little hard to talk to Mrs. Tomlin, because she didn't hear well. But once she understood she responded thoughtfully. Her fragile, lilting voice had just a trace of a Russian accent. "My husband was a doctor, a general practitioner, for twenty-eight years. We married late because he had to finish his studies.

"I was a dress designer once, but now, now I can't even hold a pencil."

If the neighbor didn't come in to put her to bed, which was often the case, she spent the night in her chair, and when the neighbor was not there to lift her to the toilet there was the humiliation of accidents. Her body was covered with bedsores.

"I tried for so many years to get someone to help me," she whispered. "Now I know I must just stay here."

A few blocks away on Barry Avenue, I pulled up in front of a light green, poorly kept house with a broken pane in the front door and paint peeling from the upper window frames. I knocked on one of the small cellar windows, and I walked around to the back entrance, through a filthy white doorway, down four concrete steps into a storage room filled with empty Coke bottles and old clothes that belonged to the family upstairs. Then, Helen Chassler, who lives in the basement, appeared in the doorway, her long gray hair pulled back into a ponytail and tied with a strip of cloth.

Helen was born in Winnetka, Illinois, on May 25, 1893, in a big brick house on the corner of Linden and Ash streets. Her father was a mathematician, her mother a Sunday School teacher who loved music. At the age of six, she was playing Beethoven, and as an adult concert pianist, she traveled around the world, and taught music for fifty years. Now she led me past the low cellar door. The bed, dresser, table, and chairs didn't disguise the fact that this was a small, unfinished basement room. There was no bathtub and no shower, just a toilet.

"It's been more than a year since I had a bath," Helen said. "See that white pan?" she added, pointing to a small porcelain pot. "It's a dishpan, but I don't use it for dishes."

When I asked about food, Helen said without any embarrassment, "Listen, do you know what it means when you haven't got a lot of money? It means that after I pay my rent I have only a few dollars left from my Social Security check and it has to last the whole month. There are many days when I eat only bread and I feel lucky that I have that."

Helen and the other people I met shared a common fate. None of them could take their next meal for granted, none of them had enough food.

Most of them didn't starve to death. The government gave them too much to die, but not enough to live. They had only one part of life. If I asked them about meat or apple pie they would shake their heads and say, "Oh, no, not for me, it's too expensive." They couldn't buy themselves a pair of shoes, a place mat, or a pound of meat. I was troubled because I knew that the condition of these people was permanent. They would die this way and then the state would dig a little hole and bury them in a potter's field.

America is a country where old people are socially isolated, tormented by ill health, and weakened by inadequate nutrition. Yet I was endlessly amazed at the richness that lay beneath their poverty.

Whenever it was possible I took my younger daughter Rebekah with me to meet these men and women. I hoped that she would listen carefully to their stories and begin to make some of the connections. I was especially glad that she was with me the day that I visited Michael Larchwood on the second floor of an old boarding hotel at 1010 Bush Street in San Francisco.

The door was open and he was waiting eagerly. He had even managed somehow to pull his trousers on over his pajamas in anticipation of our arrival. He sat on the edge of the bed in a tiny room cluttered with the memories of ninety-four years—photographs of a wife, now dead, of two sons gone somewhere, of the Marx Brothers, with whom he had once performed, and drawings he had made of the seas he had sailed. Beyond that there were a few cans of food, and an electric coffeepot without a lid in which he did all of his cooking.

"Hello, good afternoon," he said, with his voice full of pleasure. Then the tall, thin, gray-haired man held out a hand and greeted us without rising because he could not move without great difficulty.

"It's so good to meet you. It's a wonderful country we have here. It's been very good to its people. I have everything to be grateful for." The words tumbled out, perhaps because it had been so long since he'd had someone to talk to. As the afternoon wore on the outline of Michael Larchwood's life became clear. As a boy he had gone to sea. He had worked the North Atlantic on a passenger ship.

It was a time when a lot of people were traveling to North America because in those days people were given land free if they would go and live and work on it.

In 1909 Michael Larchwood took a job on the land. Then he came to San Francisco. He had always loved to sing and entertain and in 1912 he got his first engagement singing Scottish songs. It worked well and he was sent on the road. He appeared with the Marx Brothers and Sophie Tucker in vaudeville in Chicago. Then in 1914 he returned to San Francisco. He married and became a father. "I had two boys," he said, "wonderful boys. They were big, strong boys, but I don't know what happened to them. They are gone now. I think they moved to other countries." His voice dropped almost to a whisper. Then he changed the subject. He seemed not to want to remember the lonely or painful aspects of his life—which may actually have been most of it.

Cheering up, he told us he was a great believer and added that we were all made in our creator's likeness, but that *he* was born with a lucky veil. "I always start the morning with a hymn," he said, and then he recited, "'God bless you in every way and His angels watch over you day by day.' A few more years and I am a hundred. Before long God is going to take me. He's also going to take charge with His angels, and when He comes there will be no more crying, no more fighting, and no more hunger. We are just one small planet and the Creator is a blessed Creator."

He told us that even now conditions were better than they had ever been. "Think of the great rains that have taken care of our farms," he said. "Think of the oïl fields that have run our machinery." He turned to my daughter. "You are lucky, my child. You have many years left to see the wonderful things that will happen in America."

Then he looked around the room, wanting to share what little he had. "What can I give you to remember me by? I know. I'd like you to have one of my drawings." With great effort, he stood, badly bent at the waist, and moved a step or two toward his sketches. He lifted a drawing of a ship sailing strong in a storm and handed it, and a cassette recording of Scottish ballads he had made years before, to Rebekah.

Her eyes filled with tears. "Thank you, sir," she said. "Is there anything that you need, anything that I could send to you? Could I send you something for cooking?" Then glancing around the room again she said, with the candor of a child, "You have no stove, you have no refrigerator, you have no food except that soup. What do you eat?"

"Oh, I have plenty to eat," he told her smiling. "It's really very simple. You see, child, when I am hungry I just put some water in that little coffeepot and I plug it in. Then I put a can inside the pot, the water boils, and in a little while I have a nice meal.

"No, my child, I don't need anything, my little prayer takes care of it all. I am very grateful for all that I have in America." Then he gazed out his window and whistled at a bird landing on his windowsill. The bird cocked its head. "There, you see, I have a friend. I'm blessed beyond words."

4 The Politics of Hunger

The politics of hunger in America is a dismal story of human greed and callousness, and immorality sanctioned and aided by the government of the United States.

—Nick Kotz, *Let Them Eat Promises*

The old people of America who are surviving from day to day, who are poor and hungry, and living on next to nothing counted on government programs that failed them.

More and more elderly people and more and more hardworking younger people will soon find that they are in the same position, that the days of their prosperity are over. When that happens they will also find that they are treated as the poor in America have traditionally been treated by the government of the United States.

The amount and quality of government help that Americans can realistically expect, under the Reagan Administration, as the cost of food and the cost of living increase can best be predicted and understood by the government records of the past. They are records of inefficiency, corruption, and failure to reach the majority of people in need. They are records of blundering token programs at exorbitant public cost.

Nowhere is that more clearly expressed than in the history of the federally funded program designed to provide food and medical care to a group who needs it as badly as the elderly: poor pregnant women and their young children. The history of that program goes back to 1967, after Robert Kennedy stirred congressional response by reporting that he had seen families with a dozen fatherless children trying to survive on less than one hundred dollars a month. "I have seen people in America so hungry," he told the Congress, "that they search the local garbage dump for food."[6] Shortly afterward, as mentioned earlier, a Citizens' Board of Inquiry, spurred on by Kennedy, released a study that documented more widespread hunger than most congressional leaders had ever suspected. But every attempt to provide aid to those Americans resulted in failure.

The day after the report from the Citizens' Board of Inquiry had been made public, Senator George McGovern stood on the Senate floor holding a copy of the findings in his hand. On that day he introduced a motion to form the Senate Select Committee on Nutrition and Human Needs. It was to study hunger and malnutrition and the special hunger problems of pregnant women and their young children. The committee was formed, but despite its existence and the specific recommendations of the American Academy of Pediatrics, the President's Committee on Mental Retardation, and the White House Conference on Food, Nutrition and Health, years passed and no one in the government of the United States made any special provisions for pregnant women and their infants.

On August 16, 1972, the late Senator Hubert Humphrey stood where George McGovern had stood in 1967 and spoke to the Senate. He told them that the campaign to abolish hunger in America was almost six years old, and that they had continued to ignore the one group that could not speak and was most vulnerable to malnutrition.

He reminded the senators that infants, from six months prior to birth, to six months after birth, could be permanently retarded both physically and mentally because of malnutrition and that they had done nothing to assist this group.

He told them that research completed over the past six years had demonstrated beyond doubt the terrible price in physical health and mental competence that some Americans were being forced to pay because of malnutrition. As part of his plea, he brought before-and-after photographs of a young infant who had lost her struggle against malnutrition, and he passed them around the chamber. He also brought a news article from the *Memphis Commercial Appeal.* The article told of an infant, named Lucy, who was born at the John Gaston Hospital and discharged with her mother after three days. Her weight was six pounds, four ounces at birth. For all purposes she was a healthy, normal baby. But five weeks later, the baby's nineteen-year-old mother brought her to a Memphis and Shelby County Health Department neighborhood clinic. *The child had gained less than a pound since birth.* A nurse was called from the St. Jude Children's Research Hospital; on Lucy's record at St. Jude is her first impression: "Marasmic appearing child. Thin, scrawny, with protuberant abdomen, loose skin. Highly irritable." Lucy was taken to the hospital, where a pediatrician examined her and said that she was a victim of malnutrition and was on the verge of starvation. "When someone has a disease you give them medicine or a vaccination for it," he added. "Malnutrition is a disease and food is the vaccine." At first Lucy's growth increased slowly. Then she gained weight suddenly. But despite her rapid growth and new strength, Lucy's head circumference remained small. Her brain had failed to develop fully. She will be mentally retarded for the rest of her life. Nothing can reverse the process. Lucy was a victim of malnutrition. There are thousands like her in Memphis, alone; there are millions like her in the United States.

When the senators had finished learning about Lucy, Humphrey told them that he believed it was time to take the action that could end the tragic cost of malnutrition among the young. He also told his colleagues that the evidence was clear and that specific foods—such as infant formula—were available to be prescribed. He added that the only thing lacking was a system to deliver the food. He urged the Senate to step in and correct the situation, to support the amendments he proposed on child nutrition, and to endorse the amended bill overwhelmingly.

Soon afterward, the Senate did vote overwhelmingly to pass the bill and on September 26, 1972, it became Public Law 92-433. It authorized $20 million for each of the fiscal years 1973–74. The program, sometimes called WIC, for women, infants and children, was supposed to provide food supplements to poor and hungry pregnant women, and to their children up to the age of four. The legislation guaranteed health care. The program was to be administered by the U.S. Department of Agriculture. It was instructed to make cash grants to the health departments of each state; the states in turn were intended to provide funds to the local agencies.

What followed is not widely known but I believe it is worth looking at in some detail because it is representative of every congressional attempt to help the hungry of this nation. The Department of Agriculture's official and ongoing reaction to the creation of the program for hungry pregnant women and their young children was to try to destroy it. First, letters were sent to and there were negotiations with the Department of Health, Education, and Welfare to end the program. In the letters and the negotiations it was stated that WIC should end because it included a medical evaluation which the Department of Agriculture was "not organized to undertake." As a result of this dispute, five months of operating time were lost. Then USDA officials testified that none or very little of the funds could be spent in what remained of the first year because they planned to spend the time designing a "small, statistically valid medical evaluation" of the program.

Finally, eighteen months after the supplemental feeding program had been authorized and funded, the Department of Agriculture was sued in Federal District Court by a group of people who were potentially eligible for it and by organizations eager to apply for grants. The principal issue was whether former Secretary of Agriculture Earl Butz had to make the appropriated $40 million available or whether he had the discretion to reduce the amount. Everyone involved knew that Congress had intended to provide supplemental funds to as many eligible people as possible, and that from their perspective any part of the $20 million not spent in 1973 should be carried over for use in 1974.

The Department of Agriculture filed a motion to dismiss the lawsuit. It claimed that the amount of money the program would need could not be determined until it was fully operational. The Department argued that the purpose of the WIC program was not to feed large numbers of people but rather "to assemble medical data which would enable Congress to evaluate the worth of the program." They also maintained that the WIC money was part of a general pool appropriated under the School Lunch Act and the Child Nutrition Act, and claimed that meant "none of the funds earmarked for WIC purposes could be carried over to 1974, even if nothing was spent in 1973."

The court rejected each of these arguments, ruling that Congress had a twofold purpose in creating the WIC program: to help malnourished people and to secure medical data to determine whether the program should continue. On August 3, 1973, the court issued an order requiring Earl Butz to process and approve all applications that qualified for funding until $40 million, including the $20 million from 1973, were spent.

Under heavy pressure from the court, the Department of Agriculture finally promised that the first year's $20 million in still unspent funds would be carried over into the second year. But that

November, after more than three hundred clinics had applied for grants and still not received them, the battle was once again brought back to court. This time a contempt of court citation was issued against Earl Butz, and the judge ordered that all the year's grants be announced by December.

Finally, the Department of Agriculture complied.

Things appeared to be running smoothly until August 1974, when the Department of Agriculture unveiled a new plan. It required that large blood samples be taken from the jugular veins of partici- pating babies—a procedure that was both risky and traumatizing. The Children's Foundation in Wash- ington, D.C., called it "a trade-off of blood for food." And the Department could not even guarantee that well-trained people would do the testing. Dr. MaryAnn Mahaffey, city councilwoman from Detroit, said that the jugular blood test procedure "smacked of exper- imentation on the poor" and added that "such tests are not only dangerous to infants but they also dis- courage hungry people from participating in the pro- gram." The jugular blood test requirement resulted in many letters of resignation from the program. One written by an employee of the Mott Children's Health Center, representing eight Michigan health services, said that although he felt that the food was very important to his patients, he had decided that the risks were so great they outweighed the benefits.

Late in September as pressure increased, the Department of Agriculture was forced to drop the jugular blood test, but another violation soon followed. The program was supposed to publish its requirements so that applicants could tell if they qualified. Many months passed and they were not published. Again under court order, the first set of requirements was finally issued. Some of the programs were operating, but the clinics themselves were so inadequately funded that they frequently served only a fraction of their intended function.

The Bella Vista and Hawthorne Neighborhood community clinic in South Philadelphia had the lowest number of live births and the highest rate of fetal deaths in the city. For these reasons, it was among the first selected for participation in the WIC program. But eight months later, in September 1974, Maury B. Smith, the clinic's administrator, sat in his ground-floor office feeling helpless. He explained that the whole program had been a bitter disappointment. Financial restrictions had made it impossible for him to do much. He had asked for $154,000, and had gotten $52,000. At first he felt that was better than nothing. The next year the program got even less money. Maury Smith knew that the pregnant mothers needed counseling, as well as the small supply of food they were given, but he didn't have the money to hire the staff to give it to them. He feared that many women had so little money that they were trying to live entirely on this supplemental food. He wondered if the program administered this way might be doing more harm than good.

Meanwhile, in Washington, D.C., eligible women had been told that they could pick up bags of supplemental foods at ten different centers, but due to insufficient funds in 1975 this program was operating with 35 percent of its staff missing and with delivery capacities to the ten centers so inadequate that fifteen hundred bags of food went uneaten every two weeks.

Later that year in Boston, Georgia Madison, who chaired the WIC Advisory Committee for the State of Massachusetts, explained that there would be no new recipients for 1976 in Boston, even though a study conducted by the Massachusetts Department of Health indicated that only 4 percent of those women who had demonstrated that they needed the food were receiving it. Sometimes there was funding left over in a specific geographical area, but the rules were set up so that only people in that district could get the food. If you had a different zip code you could forget it, even if you were starving.

That same year I met Regina Liebowitz and Kitty Talmadge; both were pregnant and without food.

It was in Fairfax County, Virginia, the country's second richest area. But even here, emergency requests for food had become so great that the United Community Ministries and Emergency Crisis Intervention Agency, which served the Route 1 corridor, frequently found itself unable to meet the need. Located at 6206 North King Highway, this run-down, yellow cinder block building often turned people away because its own kitchen was out of food.

Sue Jacobs, the supervisor of home visits from the United Ministries, and I pulled off the highway and stopped at a dilapidated wooden house. Outside, a thin, brown dog barked at us, straining at his leash, trying, it seemed, to protect whatever little his owners had left. Flies, drawn by the dog's feces, buzzed around us as we climbed the rickety steps. Sue knocked and then opened the rusted screen door. Inside lay Regina Liebowitz, who had been living with her mother since her husband left her. Red plastic cardinals and a few plastic flowers decorated the room. Regina raised herself with difficulty when she saw us and she walked slowly and unsteadily to the brown living-room couch. She was eight months pregnant. For a moment, after she sat down, she looked just like a dozen other sixteen-year-old American girls with a freckled face and long brown ponytail.

"How long have you been without food, Regina?" Sue asked.

"Well, they took us off food stamps two months ago because my brother turned eighteen. It's been pretty rough since then. We came down here from Kentucky and when we first got here we didn't know how rough it would be. My father was supposed to give us a hundred dollars a month, but he doesn't give us anything. My husband left one night saying he was going to the store for a pack of cigarettes and he never came back. I guess he just couldn't take it, us being so poor with no work and a baby coming. Mom's out now, looking for work. So's my brother. But I'll tell you, these days work is hard to find."

"When did you last eat, Regina?" Sue asked.

"Well, I don't know, I don't remember," she said in her Kentucky accent, genuinely embarrassed by the question, her face turning deep red. "I'm not too big of an eater."

"Did you have any breakfast or lunch today?"

"I'm a real bad eater," she repeated.

Sue Jacobs handed her a bag of emergency rations and said, "Please tell your mother that when this food is gone, we won't be able to give you anymore."

"Oh, yes," she said, "I understand. I will tell her. You have been very good to us. Thank you for the food. Thank you so much."

As we drove up the highway, Sue apologized and said she hated to tell people she couldn't keep providing them with food, but that the United Community Ministries was only an emergency resource, a three-day supply, and they simply had more requests than they could handle.

We circled in behind a place called Vic's Tavern and she pointed to a group of little one- and two-room huts, explaining that the owner of this tavern allowed people with a lot of children and bad credit to live there. People who had a terrible time finding houses ended up taking these places. The rent was $250 a month for one tiny room, but often they had five kids and no place to live. They had no other choice.

The time flashed 4:30 on the Bank of Virginia clock. Just beyond it at Sherwood Hall Lane and Richmond Highway, we turned up a dirt road, and there behind the George Washington Restaurant, hidden from the view of commuters and vacationing travelers, stood half a dozen one-room shacks with no heat and no hot water.

Kitty Talmadge, who was six months pregnant, lived in one of the huts with her mother, and they were often without food. When the car pulled up, Kitty, a frail nineteen-year-old, came outside looking like an exhausted old woman. She never asked us in, perhaps because she was too ashamed of the tiny room visible through the doorway, with its rusty sink and torn sofa. But from what I could see, even if she hadn't been ashamed, there would not have been enough room for all of us to stand inside—the room was that small.

Kitty greeted us without energy, without a smile, without a word. We asked what had now begun to seem like a natural question: "Do you have any food in the house?" She did not answer. She just stared straight past us, almost through us. "Have you eaten lately?" Again, no answer. The baby needs food, we suggested, growing uncomfortable, looking for something to say. Then Kitty put her hands on her stomach and patted it very gently, sadly, with resignation, like someone who was resting after a long struggle. "Not anymore," she said, her voice trailing off, and her dark eyes growing misty. "I've been to the doctor. There is no heartbeat. Food doesn't matter to me anymore. My baby is already dead."

Meanwhile, back at the Department of Agriculture, all of the unspent government money was being poured back into the U.S. Treasury. While this was going on, Dr. Robert B. Livingston, a scientist at the University of California, San Diego School of Medicine, announced that he had developed strong statistical evidence that there were approximately two million pregnant women whose infants and young children were in serious jeopardy from malnutrition. Particularly vulnerable were brain cells. Dr. Livingston reported that infants and children living below the poverty level had unexpectedly small head circumferences. He said this provided "strong presumptive evidence for diminished brain volumes." In fact he found that the head circumferences of this population was so small that the likelihood of their constituting a normally intelligent population was less than one in a million.

Furthermore, infants and children from successively higher family income levels moved progressively nearer to normal head circumference. The brains of these deprived, hungry children weighed about a fourth of a pound less than the brains of children who were adequately fed. That brain weight difference altered their intelligence forever.

In March 1976, two months after Dr. Livingston's statement was released, the Children's Foundation in Washington, D.C. issued a press report formally announcing still another lawsuit against the U.S. Department of Agriculture. This time, the suit charged, the Department had impounded over $100 million in WIC funds. The effect of this impoundment, the announcement said, "is to keep expansion of the program to a minimum." Of the applications that were then on file to serve over half a million undernourished mothers and children, the Department planned to grant funds to no more than eighty thousand participants—or one out of every six qualified applicants. The suit was filed by the Food Research and Action Center in the U.S. District Court for the District of Columbia with the assistance of The Children's Foundation's WIC advocacy project.

The director of the project explained in March 1976 that they had worked very closely with WIC programs and applicants and had seen a lot of political pressure come to bear on the Department of Agriculture. She said that they had hoped that they would not have to go to court again. It was the third time that the Department has been brought to court regarding WIC. "Lawsuits waste time and tend to hurt the program administratively," she said, "but we have no other alternative."

Senator Hubert Humphrey spoke more angrily; he felt it was difficult to view the treatment given to the supplemental food program as reflecting anything other than another delaying tactic. Senator Humphrey believed that the Department was withholding the funds purposely with the intention of returning as much money as possible to the Treasury at the end of the year. "It may be good budget policy to authorize funds and never spend them, but it's bad health policy. High-risk mothers and infants need nutritious food supplements now while they are in a critical period of growth and brain development, and they cannot wait until after the election."

In spring 1976, Senator McGovern viewed the USDA's tactics as part of the Ford administration's attempt to appease the extreme right and emphasized that the Department had flagrantly abused its power by taking the same steps to undermine the WIC program which the federal courts had branded as illegal two years before.

Meanwhile, hundreds of thousands of hungry women, infants, and children, including the unborn, continued to be deprived of essential nutrition by the ongoing impoundment of WIC funds. In July of 1976 the courts handed down yet another decision which said the Department of Agriculture must stop holding back funds and that it must distribute them as ordered by Congress.

Then in December, Senator McGovern's committee for Nutrition and Human Needs, which had been largely responsible for holding the hearings and demonstrating that there was a problem, was dismantled. It was replaced by a nutrition subcommittee and McGovern's staff of twenty was replaced by a new staff of three.

By November 1978 WIC had been authorized to continue functioning through 1982, but new additions to the bill had made its administration far more difficult. Many communities still had no programs. The majority of those that did have programs had inadequate funding. In Pennsylvania, in the summer of 1980, State Health Department officials blamed a mistake, a malfunctioning computer system, for causing them to order a drastic cutback in their WIC program. They said that the inaccurate computer projections showed the state to be running a deficit.

This in turn caused half the agencies in Pennsylvania to freeze or cut their case loads of pregnant mothers and institute waiting lists. The officials later conceded that once the error was detected Governor Richard Thornburgh's administration waited ten months to take effective action. As a result, while infants and women went hungry, $8.5 million in unspent Pennsylvania funds were dumped back into the U.S. Treasury. Joseph H. Dunphy, a Department of Agriculture spokesman, predictably announced that the $8.5 million could not be recovered.[7]

The Department of Agriculture has conservatively estimated that 9.6 million women and children are financially eligible for and in need of the food that the WIC program provides, but as of 1980 only 1.8 million were receiving those benefits. In March 1981 President Reagan proposed to cut the case load by roughly thirty percent.

The political, economic, and social motives can be debated. The money that has been spent or returned to the Treasury by the Department of Agriculture can be calculated, but the cost of this program's failure for millions of babies born and unborn, born and mentally retarded, or born and already dead is incalculable. Agencies of the government violated a mandate assigned to them by the Congress. Well-fed administrators, executives, and lawyers argued over fine points and irrelevancies while children died.

The story of our government's failure to meet the needs of its hungry is a story that diminishes the entire nation.

No one investigating the WIC program first-hand could fail to condemn the intentional withholding of food from hungry women and children by the Department of Agriculture. The people who administer the program clearly know how badly the children need food. They know that some are starving, even starving to death, yet for the most part they have managed to keep that knowledge from the American public.

The mismanagement of the WIC program is typical. It represents a pattern in the administration of domestic food aid that has been covered up for too long. It is a pattern that must be exposed and reversed. If nothing is done, as President Reagan cuts the budget and inflation and the need for food aid increase, more and more American people will suffer.

The Food Stamp Program provides another case in point.

By 1980 a slackened economy and the exhaustion of savings had already begun to cause people of the middle class to seek aid. "We're getting more and more of the middle income group applying for food stamps now, rather than the poverty group," the supervisor of the New Orleans Food Stamp Program said in an interview. "They're a very demanding group, too, very hostile and frustrated. They don't like to have to resort to this." Federal Government officials also acknowledged that they were receiving an "increasing number of reluctant requests from men and women who once believed they had financial security and who were now full of anger and pessimism at the erosion of their purchasing power."[8] What the government officials did not say is how those people who arrived at food-stamp offices, discouraged and frightened, weary and hungry, were treated. Nor are they likely to say that the first thing people who have absolutely no food will encounter when they come to a food-stamp office is the requirement that they prove their eligibility for the program. That often takes weeks; sometimes it takes months.

At ten-thirty on a Tuesday morning, I walked into the Humboldt Park food stamp office at 2753 North Avenue in Chicago. The huge dirty room was packed full of people sitting in rows of attached plastic chairs. Each person took a number and then waited—often all day. I walked past the puffy-faced guard and sat down in the back of the room next to a tired-looking redhead with two children. She talked to me eagerly and she explained, as well as anyone I have heard, how government aid programs operate, or fail to operate. "For six months I haven't been able to get food stamps or money from the Department of Public Aid," she said. "Somehow it seems that I got on the wrong mailing list. Nobody knows why I have been cut off and nobody knows how to get me back on. Every time I come here they tell me they're still working on it. Meanwhile, I'm about to have my electricity and gas cut off. I have no money. I have no food and I have no food stamps. I have received a notice that I must move, but I have no place to go. The food stamp office has been promising me emergency stamps, but so far I haven't been able to get them either."

Our conversation was interrupted by a heavyset woman dressed in a black pantsuit. She identified herself as the "administrator of intake." Her voice was trembling with rage as she told me that no one was allowed to talk to people in the waiting room. I was led, almost pulled, from the crowded, dirty room where the hungry waited to an administrative office upstairs.

There, in a comfortable, richly carpeted office with an acoustic-tiled ceiling and padded, color-coordinated swivel chairs, I was told to wait until the administrator could find her supervisor. When I asked why the woman downstairs was left for six months without food or money, I was told that there are thirty-six variables and they must all be checked before a person can get any stamps. In order to be fair across the board we have to make sure that no client gets any special consideration. Then the woman added, "You are not allowed in the waiting room because we cannot assume people want to talk to you. We cannot play God."

When I left, entire families were sitting on the stairs that led from the administrator's office because the waiting room was so full. Many of those people would return home in the evening, still without food stamps and still without food.

The law says that if they come and have no money, they should be given free stamps for a month's supply of food, but in fact that doesn't happen. Dorothy Gartland, a nun at the Chicago Metropolitan Food Stamp Coalition and Hot Line, a private agency made up of nuns and priests who work together to help the hungry, explained, "We are here to see that people are fed. We know how badly people are treated in our public aid offices and we're prescreening them so that they know what their rights are. In our little office alone we receive three hundred calls a day from people who need help and cannot get it."

One previously middle-class man, whom I came to know in Maryland, described an experience which is typical. Jim Turner woke up at six one rainy morning; his wife and four children were still asleep. He knew that there was no way the box of rice they had on the kitchen shelf could sustain them much longer. At fifty-one, it was hard for him to admit that he had made such a mistake. Mr. Turner knew he should have asked for help sooner, but he was a man who had always taken care of himself and his family and it was very difficult for him to seek help like a poor man. He dressed quickly, then woke his wife and told her he had made up his mind to forget his pride. He was going to walk to the Social Services Office in Rockville, Maryland, and he was going to accept its help—just one check, just enough to get something into the kids' bellies. Then, somehow, they'd get on their own feet again. Turner, a small, slender man with gray hair and horn-rimmed glasses, spent most of the day at Rockville Social Services before he was told that without a doctor's report certifying that his emphysema and chronic bronchitis rendered him too weak to work, they could do nothing for him. After he told them that he didn't even have money for carfare and they told him there was nothing they could do about that, Turner walked with difficulty to his doctor's office. The doctor signed the necessary forms and added a note saying that Jim had only half of the normal lung capacity and could not possibly do any heavy work under any circumstances. But by the time the note was written, it was four o'clock and too late to walk back to Rockville before the office closed. On Wednesday, Jim returned, still on foot, and presented the doctor's note. This time he was told something that he had not been told the day before, that his wife must come back with him and sign up for a work incentive program before his request could be considered any further. So once again Jim Turner left the Social Services Office and began the walk home without money or food.

Inside the Turners' small but comfortable Montgomery County home, Carol Turner and I sat at the empty dining-room table and waited for her husband to return. Mrs. Turner, an articulate, middle-aged woman whose short brown hair was turning gray, explained that for a long time now they had been eating from day to day. Ever since the elderly woman she was taking care of died, she'd been looking for another job. She'd borrowed from the neighbors till she felt she couldn't borrow anymore.

Her daughter Leslie, a tall, slender thirteen-year-old with long brown hair, came into the room. "The kids have been very good," Carol said. "They haven't complained." Then a small blond boy with large brown eyes toddled over. Leslie picked him up. "Are you hungry?" she asked. From the refrigerator she took the last small bowl of rice and gave it to him.

The names and the faces changed but the story was the same all over America. No matter who these people were or what they had been, it was always the same struggle, the same economic vulnerability that turned the substance of life into the quest for the next meal, and it was always the same humiliating struggle with our offices of public aid.

Ironically, I often found that the men and women who grew and harvested the crops we eat could not get enough food themselves. One step down from the small farmer, homeless, and poor even when working, they were frequently victims of the worst hunger and of the worst treatment when they sought help.

I met Debra Wheeler on a large, prosperous plantation in rural Virginia. Past the acres of soybeans, past the modern farm buildings, past the splendid manor house behind the trees, I came upon a large, tumbledown, barnlike structure; inside, it had been divided into stalls smaller than those required for the horses. In one of the stalls was Debra, a fifty-three-year-old, half-black, half-Indian woman whose lung disease had made her too sick to work in the fields. Flies buzzed around a piece of rotten fruit and an empty can of Raid. It was 104 degrees.

The dust was everywhere and as she spoke Debra's coughing got worse. "I've been working in the fields picking potatoes since I was nine years old. My mother died when I was seven weeks old. Her friend raised me. She did the best she could for me, and I have always worked. Now I can't work and I can't get help."

"It's very bad this time," she said. "I have no money. I went to the food-stamp office and asked for help, but the man who is in charge there looked at me like I was a dog or something and laughed and said the man I was sleeping with could feed me. I am an old woman. I have no man. If I didn't need help, I wouldn't ask him. Everybody around here knows he treats all of us like that, but still it hurt my feelings so bad the way he was talking to me and looking at me and laughing while I was begging for food stamps."

In Virginia, as elsewhere, the food-stamp program is jointly sponsored by the U.S. Department of Agriculture and the local Welfare Department. People who qualify for the stamps can cash them in to buy food at designated grocery stores. To qualify, applicants between eighteen and sixty-five must be registered for employment with the Virginia Employment Commission unless they are already working or, like Debra Wheeler, are unable to work. I went to see the man who decided whether Debra Wheeler would eat or starve, the man who singlehandedly determined who was, and was not, eligible.

"They will lie, steal, and cheat to obtain food for tomorrow or a six-pack for tonight," said the broad-shouldered, heavyset bureaucrat with sandy hair, who peered at me over the top of his glasses. "Listen, sugar," he continued, "it's very difficult to get the truth from them. I can't lullaby them. They are not Phi Beta Kappas. We are not dealing with people who have scruples.

"In three months I personally gave away more than fifty thousand dollars in food stamps. I love this job. It's marvelous to go home and know you've helped so many people. These people are treated exceptionally well, but we can't solve their problems, so what's the use of feeding them?"

"Don't you believe that there is any way that they can be helped to better their lives?" I asked.

"Doll baby," he answered, laughing, "can you teach a cat to talk?"

Attitudes like these are not unusual; they are quite common and, in certain circles, commonly known. In an effort to reduce the cruel or impersonal treatment that most food-stamp applicants receive, the First United Church on the East-West Highway in Hyattsville, Maryland, set up a Food Stamp Coordination Center. But even the staff there was not able to do much more than be kind. The State Department of Social Services referred people to them who had heard that food stamps were available. Naturally they had many more calls than they could handle. So even people who phoned them were told to call back in a week to see if they qualified. After that they had to wait two more weeks to get an appointment at one of six churches. Then, and only then, an interviewer would go through the papers they had brought and determine with them whether or not they were eligible. Sometimes, the first time they called, people would say that they had no food and couldn't wait three weeks. When that happened the volunteers would call up the supervisors and beg for special appointments. On Fridays they always got desperate people who suddenly realized that they had a whole weekend ahead of them with no food. One little old lady accurately assessed the situation and told them what she thought. "You know, you're very nice, but it's not enough. I have no food, what am I going to do, I have no food?"

A man I met in Boston admitted that he had been arrested for stealing food. For thirty-one years David Tolanaskis had been employed as a foundry-man at Boston's Volston and Whitman Foundries. After he was laid off, he began receiving unemployment compensation. It went on for twenty-six weeks and then it stopped. He was unable to find another job. Dropping his head in shame, he whispered that he had gone into a supermarket and put a handful of cookies from a box into his pocket. "I don't believe in stealing. I know it is a crime," he said, "but I was so hungry and the markets were so full. They destroy food to keep up the prices and they don't care about the people. I go to the food-stamp office on Adams Street. I fill out the forms but I never hear from them."

The food-stamp office was supposed to provide an emergency supply of food to David Tolanaskis and to all others in a desperate situation, but it had almost completely stopped doing that. The federal government was putting pressure on the states to cut back the distribution of food stamps. It was also threatening to withhold matching funds if it discovered that ineligible people were receiving help. As a result, the food-stamp offices would not issue any stamps on a presumptive emergency basis.

The food-stamp program is not a permanent program. It has to be reauthorized by Congress every four years. In 1977 a cap was imposed on the spending. At that time the cap was thought to be adequate, but unexpected increases in the cost of food and increases in unemployment shattered those expectations. The budget office had only predicted a 2 to 3 percent annual increase in prices between 1977 and 1979; in reality, prices jumped 22 percent during that two-year period. It also predicted a decline in unemployment; instead, in 1980 we were facing an unemployment rate averaging over 6.8 percent.

Suddenly the program was grossly inadequate. There simply wasn't enough money allocated to food stamps to meet the need. Yet in March 1981 President Reagan proposed to cut 1.8 billion dollars from the food-stamp program. The suffering that this will cause cannot be calculated. As it was, in the first two months of 1981 the benefits provided to those who received stamps was only 36 cents per meal, and the median gross income of some 22 million American recipients was $3,600 per year. At that time there were 22 million Americans who needed food stamps, often literally to keep them from starving. Today, while the program is being cut, their numbers are rapidly increasing.

There has even been a rise in requests from people who are presently working but not making enough to keep up with the increasing cost of food, explained Ray Schlechter, supervisor of community services for the Philadelphia County Board of Assistance. He knows people are having a hard time, but if they do not qualify he is helpless. He's in the middle, caught between the clients and the legislators, so when these people call and tell him that they can't afford enough food to keep them from starving, he has a patent but useless answer. First he tells them that he can't help and then he suggests that they contact their legislators.

Since neither the legislators nor the administrators share the misery of the people they are serving, it is often difficult for them to understand fully what it means to be turned away. They are not in contact with extreme hardship. They do not know what it's like to return home hungry, knowing your children are hungry and that all your persistent efforts to get help and food have failed. Between breakfast, lunch, and dinner these bureaucrats may study computer printouts which identify the hungry. But they are paid whether or not food stamps are issued, whether or not people are fed. Even when a person finally meets all of the requirements and qualifies for the stamps, the administrators and legislators don't see the joy and relief of a hungry person fed. Instead, they issue paper—symbolic currency which at some other time and place can finally be traded for the food these people need to survive.

How, then, can they be expected to comprehend the impact of the decisions they make?

Kenneth Klein, the executive director of The Ark, a Jewish grass-roots emergency organization in Chicago, put it this way: "Social Security and public aid make human beings into statistics. The philosophy is, I look at your record and I don't have to see your face." He told me that Jewish Orthodox law says something very different. It says you give someone who is in need exactly what he is missing. You do what you must to get close to people. "If a man needs bread, you give him bread," Klein said. "If he needs dough to bake his own bread, you give him dough. If he needs work, you give him work. You have to face people and ask, 'What's hurting you?' The government says, 'You are coming to me as an old man or a failure.' It responds to the person as an entity with a form. They have them on a computer, but they don't know them. 'God forbid a person should get an extra meal,' says the government. 'Better he should get nothing.' "

Government programs do not have to violate the people they were created to serve. They do not have to add to the human misery and the shame that many of the hungry already feel. Recipients and applicants should not always have to be prepared for the next slur, the next rebuff, or the smug, degrading handout.

A crisis care center set up by the South Australian government in its capital city of Adelaide does what our government should be doing. It treats its hungry with sympathy and concern. It takes those who are almost overcome with despair and hunger and provides them with what they need. The program in this city of just under a million people is remarkably simple. The people who participated in the city's foster parents program were approached by government officials and asked if they would be willing to maintain a supply of food and money in their homes which could be distributed to their hungry neighbors in emergencies.

Program manager David Keer knew he had a select population. He knew that most people who will put themselves out for homeless children will also be willing to feed the hungry. These people are not paid for the work they do; only the food or money that they supply is replenished. The families are scattered throughout the city. When an emergency call is received by city officials, a telephone assessment of the needs of the person or family is made, then the

100

foster mother who lives nearest to them is contacted. Within an hour or two, or three at the most, that family will have food.

No particular method is followed; there are no charts, no forms, no computers, just a single three-by-five card with the date, the name, and the address of the person who needed food, the name of the person who provided it, and the amount that the food cost. After two years the cards are destroyed. All the funding is from the government. No private money is accepted. Each worker and each foster family is autonomous. They make an assessment and then they provide what is needed. Sometimes it is a bag of groceries taken directly from the donor's kitchen. Sometimes it is a trip to the supermarket. At other times a person in need will simply be given the cash to do his or her own shopping. It is the first emergency government food program of its kind anywhere in the world, according to David Keer. "It's simple. That is why it works; it really solves the problem."

In America, federally funded food programs have created the illusion that the problems are solved, that the hungry are provided for, but in fact they have developed rules which often make it impossible, even for the best-intentioned government employees, to meet the needs of those they are supposed to serve.

Adolph Marcus, food-stamp outreach coordinator for the city of Boston, admits that he doesn't know the solution to the problem. He gets calls all the time from people who say they have no food, and they have no stamps, and there is nothing he can do about it. He cares about people and he is deeply troubled by his inability to help them. He's been in the food-stamp program since 1963 and says that things have gotten progressively worse. He now gets countless requests from people who do not meet all of the requirements for emergency food stamps and yet have no food. If they are on welfare, he refers them back to their caseworkers; if not, he suggests the Salvation Army. They can *sometimes* give something.

"I'm in no position to help," he explains sadly. "I can't give the stamps away. Help, even for the desperate, must come from another source."

II

The Threat of Increasing Hunger

American consumers can look forward to higher prices both for staples like bread and for meat, poultry and dairy products, which are indirectly produced by using feedgrains. . . The trends followed in the past years, if continued, could lead us straight to disaster.

—Paul R. Ehrlich
The End of Affluence

5 America's Vulnerable Farmers

If all food production were to stop today, no fresh milk would be available tomorrow. Eggs and red meat would be gone in five days, chicken in seven, and within a month all dried and condensed milk would have been sold. Supermarkets would have only a three- to five-day food supply which could be wiped out within hours.
                    —Jules Archer, *Hunger on Planet Earth*

The government of the United States turns countless numbers of eligible and hungry people away from existing food programs without food or the immediate hope of getting any. . . . It abandons

millions of elderly people who have paid money into
the Social Security system through all their working
years to live in hunger and poverty. . . . It allows
millions of pregnant women and infants to be
severely undernourished and some to starve and die
while pouring available funds back into the U.S.
Treasury. . . . Marasmus and kwashiorkor, diseases
of extreme protein and calorie deficiency thought to
exist only in underdeveloped countries, are found in
the United States today. All in a time of affluence.

The government of the United States has
proven itself to be unable to meet the need. It does
not have the working programs, the priorities, nor
the judgment to cope with the people in America who
are hungry now, let alone the will to deal with an
agricultural crisis.

That potential crisis is the second concern of
this book. It is also, of course, the common factor that
could, quickly and without warning, link the lives of
the fortunate to the lives of the unfortunate. The
concept of widespread hunger in the midst of so
much abundance at first seems unthinkable, almost
laughable. It is always especially difficult to antici-
pate things that have never occurred, to see and
respond to the converging elements of a larger
pattern before it is upon us.

Nevertheless, over the past decade that pattern
has become increasingly clear. I think it comes to
this: The poor feel the shortages and the rising costs
first, but the effects of ongoing carelessness and
abuse and poor planning will slowly filter down to
the rest of us. It is no longer safe to assume that the
awful suffering hunger brings will stay in circum-
scribed places and not spill over into all our lives.

In order to find out how vulnerable the food
supply in America really is or if a crisis could occur

without warning and suddenly leave millions of completely unprepared Americans without enough food or the hope of getting it, I began the second part of my research. I flew to Nebraska, the heart of America's farmland.

I rode the tractors and walked the rich, abundant cornfields. I talked to the farm advocates and farmers. From them I learned how crucial the land is to all of us. I learned something about the social, political, and economic burdens that undermine the food-producing structure of this nation. I also observed how these people live. Some of them told me what they feared and perceived about the future of family farms and about the future of America's food supply. I spoke to farmers who were going bankrupt, to farmers who were "getting by," and to farmers who had grown rich.

While there was no "representative" farmer, people in certain economic categories did seem to have particular kinds of concerns. I found that American farmers were more alike than different. They were all people who worked directly with the land and watched it produce the food that most of us never see until much later when it is on the shelves of our supermarkets, packaged or frozen or canned.

Most of the farmers I spoke to were people who had given a lot of themselves to the earth, and with great respect, almost reverence, had watched it give back, or try to give back, something to them. Most had seen the changes in the American food supply directly reflected in that earth. They had seen the earth respond to the pressures of the economy and the demand to produce more and more, faster and faster. Often under economic pressure and against their better judgment they had applied chemicals to the soil and to the living things that they grew. Most had also switched to larger and larger machines and more and more sophisticated methods of stressing the earth and increasing the amount of food it could yield. They had lived through the period of America's greatest abundance. Some had ridden its crest and grown rich; others could not compete and grew so poor they went hungry themselves.

Whatever the changes in agriculture and productivity meant to them, they were now seeing the start of a new era: an era of diminishing crop yields, increasing oil dependency, and frantic new combinations of chemicals. They were all experiencing an increasing sense of dread.

From those men and women who work the land and love it, I heard about the almost impossible struggle of the small farmer to survive and produce good food and compete without expensive, sophisticated machinery. I also learned something of the little understood, long-range dangers of replacing family farms with large, corporate farms. Some spoke of the anguish and fear of being driven off the land they farm and thus prevented from doing the work they have done all of their lives, the work they love and the only work they know how to do.

I heard about the painful choice made by those with middle-sized farms to destroy their land's future productivity by overplanting and overusing chemicals rather than being economically destroyed themselves right now. Some who had been abusing the land longer watched helplessly as their soil grew barren and their crop yields dropped.

Most of all, American farmers spoke of their fear of running out of the fuel they used in every aspect of farming, of not being able to make their machinery run, of watching this rich land grow poor and hunger spread across the cities and villages of America.

Almost without exception there was a great sense of change and of loss, a sense that something was very wrong in American agriculture and that it was growing worse.

On a hot Tuesday in June, I crossed the main street of the tiny Nebraska town called Walthill. I walked past an abandoned furniture store and an abandoned hotel, and I stopped in front of a small storefront library open three hours a week. I learned that farm towns like this one were littered all across the United States. The decay in these towns reflected the decay in farming and the fact that the agricultural wealth of these American communities was being siphoned away.

I arranged a meeting with Judy and Richard Dye, small, hardworking farmers who, like millions of others, were slowly being driven out of business and off the land. I wanted to know what it was like for them, but I was also concerned about what the loss of the family farmers would mean to us, the American people.

At the town's only cafe' I met Judy Dye, a heavyset blond woman of about forty, whose blue sweat shirt proclaimed *I'm Proud to Be a Farm Wife.* We shook hands and she asked, a little too cheerfully, "What can I tell you about going bankrupt?" Later, as we drove to her farm in a battered blue pickup, we got past the veneer of optimism. Judy explained that her husband had owned their farm for twenty-five years. When they were married fifteen years before, she came to live on the farm with him and his father. The land that they farm is glacial deposit land. It is sandy and marginal. At first in order to compete they started investing in lots of fertilizers and chemicals, but they were putting in more than they were getting

109

out. So they turned to organic farming. They used fertilizer, but only organic fertilizer. They refused chemicals because they found that after a while they lost the humus in their soil and the chemicals no longer did what they were supposed to do.

When they began farming hay, they had four people working for them. They had developed their own markets, and they were operating a reasonably profitable hay farm. Then a sudden change in government policy caused the price of hay to drop from seventy-five to thirty dollars a ton. It was costing them forty-five dollars to produce each ton.

"We quickly went broke," Judy explained. "We lost in one year what we had built up in many. At first we couldn't understand why it had happened. Then we learned that the government was trying to get the price of corn up. They were paying seventy to eighty dollars a ton for corn and causing the value of hay to drop. We tried to switch over to corn but it was too late. For us it was all over. Our expenses were high and we didn't have any cash. We had to borrow a hundred percent of what we needed. We borrowed the limit from the Farmers Home Administration at eight percent interest, but it wasn't enough to get a new crop going. Meanwhile we kept trying to pay them back, and each year we found ourselves deeper in debt. Now we owe them fifty thousand dollars."

We turned in at a dirt driveway and stopped in front of a small, poor farmhouse with a tar-paper roof badly in need of repair. A black puppy rolled in the mud in front of the doorway. Inside the run-down kitchen a blond-haired child of about ten was industriously baking bread which, I was told, she sold in town to supplement the family's income.

Richard Dye, a big, burly, plainspoken man in a gray work shirt and patched overalls rolled up at the ankles, sat in his living room on an old tweed chair; his toes pushed through the holes in his gray socks. He leaned back in the chair and said slowly, "It's the problem of trying to keep a free enterprise going. We can get people better-quality food if we can keep farming. Our dream is a simple dream. What we want more than anything is just to grow and process our own corn, but here's the problem. To do that we need a large huller and a grinder. Things have gotten bad—in fact, they have gotten very bad—and we know that without this machinery we just can't compete. With it we would grow corn and process our own and other farmers' grain. Sometimes I think that we could even start a small corporation and set up shares. But without the machinery we are just trying as hard as we can to keep our farm. Since we have no money, the Farmers Home Administration controls all that we can do. We asked over and over for a loan to buy a huller and grinder or a used combine, but each time they said no. The emotional strain of dealing with them has been pure hell. In the process we have grown so poor that now we're on food stamps," he added.

"Ironic, isn't it?" Judy added. "The people who grow America's food have to get food stamps."

Then she noticed me looking past the single end table to the bedroom. There was no bed, just a mattress on the floor. "As you can see, we have no bed, we have next to nothing. Fortunately, I understood that land was not a liquid asset. If I hadn't been knowledgeable about that we wouldn't have been able to qualify for the food stamps. Come on," she said, trying to be cheerful, "let me show you the rest of the place."

Outside again, we made our way through thick mud, past a thin-looking cow and a few chickens, to a trailer that had housed their farmhands in the better days. Inside the trailer Judy Dye ground a bag of cornmeal in a small wooden grinder. "This is called a magic mill," she explained. "It cost two hundred eighty-five dollars. We can grind sixty pounds of meal an hour with it, but we can't use it to compete with the big farmers. We're at the point where we've just about given up trying to qualify for an equipment loan. Many farmers still have the illusion that they have control over what they do. It used to be that way, but the truth is that today the small farmer has very little control."

Later as we drove back to town Richard Dye clarified what Judy had said. "It was the self-sufficiency and the pride of the people that made this country. Now the big corporations with their technology and their chemicals have taken over the whole system. Free enterprise is being trampled on, and if you take that away there isn't a heck of a lot left. We've tried hard to diversify our crops; we've also tried to develop some unique concepts which we hoped would compensate for the large-scale machinery we couldn't afford, but now we feel as if it's hopeless. Every year, as more and more corporations have come in, things have gotten worse for us. Farms like mine go out of business bit by bit and the farmers who love them die in little pieces."

Richard Dye is not every small farmer and yet he is doing more than describing himself. There are hundreds of thousands of farmers in his position today, good, hardworking men who began with a dream and watched helplessly as it was destroyed. Many are feeling the things that he is feeling, wanting more than anything just to work the land and grow the best food they can. The rate at which these farmers are driven off the land will increase radically if President Reagan's proposed 25 percent cut in loans to farmers goes into effect in 1982.

So far, no one has made a connection between the lives and losses of these farmers and the lives and losses of the hungry people who need the food that the farmers are prevented from producing. Certainly there is some spiritual connection in their suffering, their frustration, and their poverty. But I think there is a more practical, direct measurable connection. I think that there is even a connection between the bankruptcy of these farms and the growing difficulty that the American middle class is experiencing with the rising cost of food.

Contrary to general belief, large farms are not more energy-efficient than small farms. Federal figures indicate that small farms actually outproduce large farms. When the production costs are added to the costs of transportation, storage, processing, packing, and handling, the difference in costs between the large-scale production and distributor operation and the small-scale farmer—using fewer machines, no artificial chemical products, and selling locally—will become very evident. Part of the reason that the consumer is receiving less and less food for every dollar spent is directly linked to the fact that the small farmer is being driven out. Large farms that are totally dependent upon ever more expensive energy must, in turn, charge the consumer more. In some cases the rate of application of petrochemical fertilizers alone is five hundred pounds per acre. As the soil deteriorates, as much as 50 percent of that fertilizer is leeched away. Residues often contaminate domestic water systems.[9] In the short run, yields and profits may increase, but in the long run the land and the economy are permanently damaged.

113

Most Americans feel secure even though they know that the small farmer is being driven out. They aren't worried about who grows the food, as long as they can get it. But that sense of security is not firmly grounded because large-scale production and distribution networks that are replacing the small farmers are totally dependent on petroleum fuel and other nonrenewable resources. A three-week disruption in fuel accessibility could cause a year's supply of food to be lost. A longer disruption could destroy agriculture as we know it in America today.

America has taken an agrarian system that was based on human labor and turned it into a food-producing system that relies on depletable resources that are becoming more and more difficult to get. At the same time, the farmers who took care of the soil and loved it are being replaced by investors who are not only absent but also disinterested and careless.

When America abandoned the preservation of the family farm as a social objective, it destroyed a heritage that had served it well. It sacrificed a tradition, it destroyed the dream that an honest hardworking man could make his way in a good free society and replaced it with a system where only the people who don't have to own land can afford to.

Americans have been told that 96 percent of our manpower has been "freed" from food production. However, they have not been told how many of those Americans did not want to be "free" or how many struggled and fought to maintain their farms.

If the trend continues over the next twenty years, between 200,000 and 400,000 small farmers like Richard Dye will lose their farms each year. At first those numbers appear to contradict farm statistics gathered by the 1980 census which reported a stabilizing pattern of farm ownership. But the

114

census is now defining a farm as any place from which "1,000 or more dollars of agricultural products were sold or normally could have been sold in a year."[10]

The truth is that this nation's exclusive emphasis on production has forced farmers to get larger or to get out. Too few Americans have asked what the human and the agricultural price will be, or ultimately what the effect will be on the cost and supply of food for the average American.

Less than a hundred years ago this country promised a new way of life. Farmers believed that success was linked to honesty, hard work, and individual effort. In losing the system based on those concepts, and in losing the long-enduring families who cared for the soil, America is also giving up the stability of a long-term, reasonably priced food supply. We are replacing it with a system that has often been called the envy of the modern world, a system by which one farmer can feed himself and fifty-six others if the soil holds out and *if* he has oil.

Every day 200,000 barrels of oil are used to manufacture nitrogen fertilizer—over 100 million barrels of oil a week just to keep pace with current demand. For every calorie of food produced, 6.4 calories of energy must be expended. By the time that a calorie of food has been processed, as much as 15 calories of energy may have been consumed. In some cases it has been estimated that the tractors used to prepare a field burn up as much energy as the entire field can yield.[11]

That one American farmer can now feed himself and fifty-six other people has been made possible by the substitution of nonrenewable energy sources for human labor. This "accomplishment" has been accelerated by a collaboration among large corporations, government agencies, industrialists, and bureaucrats.

The large corporate farms are no longer places to live. They are systems of production. They carelessly draw upon the limited resources essential for maintaining human life and blithely hope for some new technological breakthrough that will remedy the damage. Fields are losing their topsoil, groundwater tables are becoming chemical swamps polluted with pesticides and herbicides that are absorbed through the soil, and farmers can compete only if they get bigger and bigger tractors and use more and more chemicals.

Often, becoming a large enough farmer to stay in business means destroying the soil's future capacity to produce food. Most farmers know how to take care of the soil. They know, for example, that plowing in the fall causes erosion from wind all winter long, whereas leaving a stubble from last year's crops prevents the topsoil from blowing away. Yet farmers are plowing in the fall to save time in the spring. Abuses tend to be worse on the bigger farms because they have more land to cultivate.

The farmers who have survived have become dependent upon technology. They have figured out how to use irrigation and chemicals and machinery to make the land produce a huge amount of food for what they know will be a limited number of years, but they haven't figured out how limited. "Continuous corn" is the phrase most commonly used in Nebraska. American farmers know that "corn on corn" is bad for the soil, but often they think only of the moment and the short-term profits.

Ned Thompky, a handsome, vigorous man in his seventies, has been growing corn continuously for twenty-four years. He is a successful Nebraska farmer. Economically he does well—better than 95 percent of all the farmers in America. Thirteen years ago he lost his arm in a new machine he had not yet learned how to use, but he accepted the loss as part of the price of progress and kept right on buying the newest machinery without worrying about the risks. He put in the first central pivot irrigating system in his area. The neighbors didn't like it; they were afraid that it would pump the earth dry but it seemed to work miracles. With it, Ned Thompky was able to plant his corn three times thicker than theirs and that gave him enough money to expand. Today he owns six pivot irrigation units worth fifty thousand dollars each and rents three more. Some of the neighbors are still upset about the pivot systems, but now they are also worried that without such systems of their own, they will be unable to compete. They fear that they will go broke and that Thompky, who has already gone from 160 inherited acres to 2000 acres, will buy them out. Thompky hired an agronomist who tells him how much nitrogen, how much sulfur, and how much potash it will take to produce 150 bushels of corn per acre. It takes a lot more now than it used to, but so far it still seems to be working. So do the giant pivot irrigating systems.

"They're pretty nice deals," Thompky told me, smiling proudly, pointing to the metal structures with one-quarter-mile-long swinging arms and ten sets of wheels that rotate over 160 acres of ground every twenty-four hours. The water sprayed on the crops is pumped from the ground 140 feet below and then mixed with nitrogen from a giant tank before it reaches the earth. The land, of course, has been stripped of ground cover and trees and shelterbelts to make room for the movement of the arm.

The nitrates that are used on the corn are being absorbed through the soil, back into the aquifers from which drinking water is supplied. So far it hasn't made the Thompkys sick. However, a cow did die from nitrate poisoning on a nearby ranch and some of the neighbors are starting to worry because when nitrates get into groundwater they stay there. According to Dr. Ray Spalding, a water-quality expert from the University of Nebraska, between 1975 and 1976 irrigators had almost doubled their use of nitrogen and nearly 50 percent of that nitrogen was being leached directly into the water supply. Twenty percent of the irrigation wells in the Nebraska area now contain concentrations of nitrogen that considerably exceed the Board of Health limit of ten milligrams per liter. Dr. James Ramsey of Atkinson, Nebraska, and Dr. William Becker of Lynch say that they have treated a number of area residents for nitrate poisoning.[12]

But the Thompkys aren't worried about that.

When I asked Ned Thompky if he was concerned about pumping the earth dry and using chemicals or if he thought the soil would be ruined and unable to produce food in the future, he answered, "The only thing that's worrying me is being *cut off* from our chemicals. You see, without them there would be no way for us to farm." And then he added, "Those chemicals require fuel to produce. Without fuel we lose our chemicals right away. Without fuel we can't run the irrigating systems. Without fuel we can lose a whole crop easy within a single week. The truckers block those pipelines for two or three weeks and it's all over. Not just our crop, *everybody's* crop. We got spoiled because in the past it has been so easy to get on the phone and tell the supplier to bring a thousand gallons; it has always been delivered and we've always taken it for granted. Our giant combine cost seventy-five thousand dollars. With it we can plant corn all night and if something goes wrong the light just starts a-blinking. But it won't do a thing without fuel. Our yellow grain was sold to the West Coast for export but it can't be moved without fuel. To be big farmers we need the fuel and we need the phosphate. We can't get along without them."

Then Thompky's voice lowered in concern as if he were sharing a secret with me. "I am told that in America we've used up all our good phosphate deposits already. Now we are on the second-grade deposits. That means they practically used up all the known deposits. It takes more energy to get the little that's left, and energy itself is growing more expensive and harder to get every day." The old gentleman with the white hair and the twinkling blue eyes shook his head and said, "Right now, I'm happier than I've ever been in my life, but I don't know where it's going. You understand, I didn't think I would see this much change in my lifetime. I never thought I'd have a combine or use herbicides. Yes, I have to admit it, sometimes I worry a great deal, but then I just remind myself that everything is going in our favor. Once we had burrs all over our land, then we got those chemicals, 2,4-D and 2,4,5-T; you know, in Vietnam they called it Agent Orange. We spray it and it kills the burrs," he laughed. "There you go. It's wonderful with those chemicals; we've got a wonderful country here.

"No one can raise corn as well as we can," Thompky told me. The corn creates the beef and the pork and the poultry, even the sugar. "It's only the fuel problem, the energy that we seem to be running out of. But we'll get that solved, yes, I know that we'll get that solved. I see only good years."

119

As fear merges with denial, the hopes of the large-scale farmers and technological optimists center on the belief that technology, like magic, extends itself indefinitely and that the soil can continue to renew itself no matter how much it is abused. Of course the farmers have been told and they know that single-crop farming destroys the balances that the earth uses to renew itself. They realize that it increases the need for more and more expensive petrochemicals, both to augment the natural substances destroyed by single-crop planting and to kill specific strains of insects that otherwise would not have multiplied and grown hardy. At some level all of the farmers I spoke to felt that the industrialization of agriculture, which appeared to solve the problems of food production, had at once both spurred and masked the long-term threat to the food supply.

In terms of energy, America has the world's least efficient farming system. Our advanced agricultural technology requires five to ten calories of fuel to obtain one calorie of food. This is in stark contrast to primitive cultures which still obtain five to fifty food calories for each calorie of energy invested.[13] America's farmers are among the most energy-dependent groups in today's economy. That makes them and the American food supply among the most vulnerable to changes in the cost and supply of petrochemicals.

The changes in American food production have occurred so rapidly that Leonard Scholten, a South Dakota farmer who was born in 1910, still remembers when *all* of the farming was done with horses.

I talked to him about what the changes meant and what he thinks they will lead to. We reminisced a bit and he told me that as a boy it was his job to feed the horses. In those days all the corn was picked by hand. When he was in the eighth grade Leonard drove six-horse wagons and a two-dobbin plow. Then in 1928 his family got its first tractor. After that, everything changed quickly. When he was a small boy the whole family was needed to farm. Everyone would get up at six o'clock, have breakfast while the horses ate, then Leonard would go out and milk the cows. After that he'd help his father separate the cream from the milk. Then they would tend the grain or harvest the feed. They'd take a nap for an hour and then they'd go out and harvest some more, until six o'clock at night. Before they knew it, there it was, time to milk the cows and feed the horses again. It was hard work. There was no doubt about that. It wasn't always pleasant and yet it was a way of life and a way of belonging.

When the machines and the chemicals came, farmers began to experience a certain freedom that they had never known. At first they loved it. Leonard Scholten said he had never been nostalgic about the past until the last few years; then slowly he began to wonder. It began to seem to him as if another kind of enslavement was taking over. Back in 1940 land in his area was $40 an acre. Now, it's $1500 or $1600 an acre. To make a lower-middle-class income today a farmer needs 500 acres and $150,000 worth of equipment.

"My son Harry and I farm together. We have had to make some hard choices," Leonard Scholten said. "We have pathetic, obsolete, broken-down facilities for our livestock. We can't even afford to repair our barn. But we have all of the advanced equipment, including a turbo 770 combine with an air-conditioned cab."

At that point Harry, a tall, thoughtful, dark-haired man in his thirties, joined the conversation. Trained as an aerospace engineer, he had given up that career because of something he had remembered about the freedom of a man who worked close to the earth. But he found that farming wasn't what he had expected it to be. "Sometimes it seems like I'm not a farmer at all," he admitted, "but a man-machine combination, a portable operating unit. Every nickel of expendable income I get goes back into the machinery so that I can make it again the next year. And those little chemical sprayers I have on my planter," he added, openly showing his distress as he took me on an equipment tour, "they spray herbicides. It's economic necessity."

Harry knows what's good for the soil but he can't do it without going out of business. "I am told that we've lost half of the organic matter in our soil," he confided. "I know I am going headlong into things I am not sure about, that might have consequences I can't predict, but if I don't do them I couldn't farm. Soil is a living system and it's being looked at as a chemical system. I have no way of knowing what I'm doing to the microlife of the soil. It's so easy to become confused. It's so easy to do horrible destruction to things we don't want to destroy. I don't like to just do things, I like to understand."

The concerns that Harry and his father expressed are typical of countless American farmers who know that they are getting by—at a price.

For them, there is a sense of bereavement, a sense of something worse than the economic struggle. There is the pain of knowingly injuring the land they love, the land they want to care for, and know how to care for, and yet can't care for without destroying themselves.

For the American people there will also be a price: land ruined beyond repair, land unable to produce the food we will need in the future.

"Why do you stay?" I asked Harry.

"I stay in this work because every now and then I can still touch the earth—even if I have to climb out of my combine to do it. No matter how much technology there is, no matter how much damage we do, I can still feel the rain on my face and get a sense of what the world is or should be like." Then, he added, perhaps baffled by his own devotion, "I guess I'm willing to give up a lot for that."

He has given up a lot. Harry's whole image of a free, hardworking man providing his family with security and comfort in an old farmhouse has died. As we talked, we walked toward what had once been a beautiful, white clapboard farmhouse—until 1972 when faulty wiring had caused a serious fire. Because there was no money available to repair their house, the Scholtens moved out. Home had become little more than an extension of the machines themselves, a prefabricated trailer.

The older Mr. Scholten led me into the house. At first it looked like nothing but abandoned rubble, but then I noticed the fresh pot of coffee sitting on the only counter that had not been destroyed by fire.

"This is still home to me," Leonard Scholten said softly, almost apologetically, and then he paused, raising his gray eyes questioningly, tentatively wondering if I would be willing to join him there in what remained of his house. I nodded yes as he offered me a cup of coffee. Then, encouraged by my acceptance of the place, and of him, he took out three aluminum chairs from somewhere and he, his son, and I sat down to talk in the middle of the burned-out kitchen.

"I guess this old farmhouse symbolizes all that has been destroyed for us since agriculture changed," Leonard Scholten said gravely. "We are farming a million dollars' worth of investment, five hundred and forty acres of land. We are feeding sixty to seventy people with the food we are producing and yet we are living closer to subsistence than we care to admit."

"How would you feel about going back to the way it was when you were a child—as we would if we ran out of fuel?" I asked, inaccurately sensing that he would prefer to return to the earlier ways. Despite the painful position he was in, Mr. Scholten found my question unthinkable.

"We're talking about survival. Not just *my* survival as a farmer, but survival and food for the *entire* country. Survival—that is really what is at issue. If we couldn't get the fuel, we'd have to let everything go to grass, we would have no way to till. None at all. We'd have to farm with a stick. Eventually we'd go back to animal technology, but we'd have to relearn it and train the horses. You couldn't just get the horse economy going overnight. You can't even farm with horses until they are four years old. No," Leonard Scholten said, "you couldn't do it fast enough with horses to keep the country from starving. We are beyond the point of no return. Yet, it's so hard to get oil sometimes and so expensive, and I hear we're running out of it. It could happen. Corn alcohol could be used in an engine," he added thoughtfully, "but it's inefficient and it would take seventy-five percent of our land just to produce the corn to use for our fuel."

Harry looked at me hard, then he asked in his plainspoken, direct way, "Are you aware that the East Coast is at the end of the food chain? Do you know that *everything* you people in the East eat comes in on a truck and that everything we sell goes out on a truck? Without adequate fuel most American cities would get to the point where you couldn't live in them anymore. Without adequate fuel, farmland would become ranchland and ranchland would have to be abandoned." Without waiting for an answer he continued: "My own ability to produce would drop ninety percent. I could feed my family and that's about it. If it happened for any length of time I doubt if we'd ever get back from subsistence. We are much more interrelated than most people think. To survive we need to provide food and to produce food we need the fuel, the truckers, the diesel, the whole ball of wax. What frightens me is knowing that with a population of two hundred and thirty million people in America we could not survive without fuel. Twenty-five million could make it, but the other two hundred five million would starve to death except for the ones who shot each other first in an effort to get food."

I left the Midwest the next morning wondering if the leaders of the country knew the things that I had learned from these people, or if they were genuinely unaware of how unstable the foundations of American agriculture were. I returned home to the East, to the biggest gas crisis the United States had ever experienced.

As I waited in the two-and-a-half-block gas line in a Philadelphia suburb, my thoughts shifted to an image of lines like these gas lines outside of our supermarkets. I pictured women with babies waiting from 8:00 a.m. to 4:00 p.m. for a rationed five-dollar supply of food only to be told that the supermarkets had just run out and would be closed until the next day. I envisioned newspapers printing lists of open food stores instead of open gas stations. My thoughts were broken by a passing police officer who had been assigned to keep peace in the gas lines since a number of shootings over fuel for cars had begun to cause panic throughout the East. "Stop driving your cars," he ordered, waving his arms, "leave them in your garages." Many of us could do that fairly easily for a week or two, I thought. But how long could we last without food? Five days? A week? Two weeks?

6 Food or Heat

*Symptoms of the crisis will begin to appear long
before the crisis point is reached. Food prices will rise
so high that some people will starve to death.*
—Club of Rome, *The Limits to Growth*

Viola Pickens stood in an alleyway on Chicago's
South Side holding her infant granddaughter. It was
December but the sun was shining and they had
come outside to try to get warm. She and the infant
and her fourteen-year-old son lived in a small rear
apartment that was so cold and so damp that mold
covered the walls like wallpaper. When I saw them

they had been without heat all winter. She said she had given up. She didn't even dream about heat anymore and then she told me why.

"The price of oil is so high that it is a choice between a little heat—not even enough to keep us warm—and food. Not good food, but enough to keep us going. It's cold. It's very cold. Some nights it is so cold I don't know if we can last till morning. But one thing I do know, we can't stay alive without food. So I tell my son we really have no choice and we have to try it this way and not complain and blame each other and make it worse. So we dress very warm and we stay near the stove. We do the best we can . . . we pray.

"I know it's not good for the baby and when they are small like this they just cry and cry and there's nothing you can tell them that will help to make them understand. Sometimes I put the baby's face under my coat and I rock her like that till she falls asleep. Like I said, I know it's much too cold in here for her, but I don't want to put this child in a foster home. It would hurt me so bad and I don't even know how much good it would do. I heard Jimmy Carter say that everybody's running out of oil—the whole country, even the rich people—so I figure it's really no use to part with the child because we're just the first and no one's going to have oil for long."

Viola Pickens was talking about a speech that a grim Jimmy Carter made to the nation on April 18, 1977, a speech that frightened her and a lot of other people in the cities as much as it had frightened the farmers who knew that without oil they couldn't produce food. Viola Pickens wondered how long her family could survive if the trend continued or intensified. "The United States relies on gas and oil to run three-fourths of the economy," Carter had said, "and we are running out of it. The energy crisis has not overwhelmed us yet but it will if we do not act quickly."

Until recently most Americans had never worried about the supply of oil running out. "Supply" was something that farmers and politicians and industrialists and consumers didn't concern themselves with. Then suddenly we were told we had reached a point where the issue of "supply" could no longer be ignored or forgotten. We had to deal with it because for the first time in United States history the possibility of starvation in America could literally depend upon what Jimmy Carter had characterized as "a thin line of oil tankers stretching halfway around the earth to one of the most unstable regions of the world."

After listening to Jimmy Carter's speech and speaking to American farmers about their fears and to Viola Pickens about hers, I decided to try to trace the roots of the energy crisis and to determine for myself how it would affect the American food supply.

I knew, as we all knew, that until the 1960s the United States had produced all of the oil it needed. I also knew that by 1980 the difference between the oil we produced and the oil we used was almost seven million barrels a day. Forty-one of every hundred barrels we consumed were imported. It was clear that unless consumption was brought into balance with production the United States would remain dangerously vulnerable to disruptions in supply. But it was not clear to me that we were really running out of oil.

The best information on the subject that I came across was an investigative series written by Pulitzer Prize winning-reporters Donald L. Bartlett and James B. Steele. It was published in the *Philadelphia Inquirer* and it pointed out that Representative

Richard J. Welch (R., Calif.) told his concerned colleagues in the House of Representatives that known petroleum deposits amounted to twenty billion barrels of crude oil and that at present rates of consumption U.S. known reserves would be exhausted in less than twelve years. However, that was in *1947*.

Since then the United States has produced more than five times the amount of oil we were told we had. In 1981 the estimate for proved reserves was 7.1 billion barrels higher than it had been in 1947.

Proved reserves are defined as oil that has already been located. They have little to do with how much oil there actually is. The *Inquirer* series also pointed out that there was reason to believe that the amount of American oil made available and the amount produced is not related to supply but is, instead, directly related to the price at which it can be sold. Even now with oil prices decontrolled, the amount of money the companies can make keeps rising so it is often more desirable for American companies to "discover," produce, and sell their oil later. This practice increases the power of the Organization of Petroleum Exporting Countries (OPEC) nations and the vulnerability of the American people.

The Saudi Arabian oil minister has warned the U.S. Senate that even if there is no disruption in supply by 1982, "oil shortages in America will be chronic. They will be deep and of long duration."

The Saudi government has increased the price of oil 1500 percent since 1972—from two dollars to more than thirty dollars a barrel. The United States has accepted each price increase, and as a result the people of this country have suffered greatly.

Today this nation's entire economy and agricultural structure are unprotected against more and more unreasonable price increases or a cutoff in supply; to offset the danger, Congress had set a deadline of December 1978 for stockpiling 250 million barrels of oil. But the oil companies failed to do it. In 1980, after five years of effort, the reserve held only 102 million barrels, the equivalent of a fifteen-day emergency supply of imported oil.

Even if the OPEC countries use restraint in price increases, and conservation reduces demand, the price of domestic oil will continue to rise now that price controls in the United States are lifted. As that happens the price of food will also rise. Not only is the government of the United States doing nothing to prevent this from happening, it is actually making decisions that ensure that America's problems will become increasingly pervasive, decisions that guarantee that food prices will rise so high that many who are getting by today will go hungry in the near future.

Because the government is unwilling to oppose the powerful vested interests of the energy suppliers, here and abroad, it is making the kinds of choices that, at best, will cause severe increases in the cost of food and, at worst, will lead the country to economic and agricultural disaster. Energy fraud and corruption are rampant. Energy bills enacted between 1978 and 1980, which were designed to "solve" the energy problem, were actually the start of what is probably the most expensive legislative boondoggle in the nation's history.

In June 1980 Congress passed the Energy Security Act and created the U.S. Synthetic Fuels Corporation. That corporation now has the power to hand out $88 billion for "testing" synthetic fuel plants between 1980 and 1990. However, the nation already has workable synthetic plants. It has had them for years. In Rapid City, South Dakota, a workable pilot plant successfully turned coal into gas in 1972. It is closed and shuttered today. So is another pilot plant in Princeton, New Jersey, that successfully turned coal to oil in 1972. And another in Bruceton, Pennsylvania, that was working well in 1975. In addition, there are more than half a dozen other synthetic fuel plants that have been proven successful and then been closed and abandoned. In fact, back in 1947 an internal memorandum circulated in the U.S. Interior Department predicted that within four or five years the synthetic fuels industry could produce two million barrels of petroleum products each day. Now, after four decades of research, the government predicts that the industry will only be able to meet one-tenth of the goal it set in 1947.

The truth is that the techniques for creating synthetic fuels are not dependent on any new technological breakthroughs. The technology has been known and has been used in England for almost two hundred years.

The billions that will be allocated to more and more pilot programs and more and more demonstration plants are, quite simply, a highly lucrative method of stalling. The nation's largest oil companies have no intention of marketing synthetic fuels or making them available until they will offer the largest possible profits.

The then Energy Secretary James R. Schlesinger openly acknowledged the issue in April 1979. He said, "The real question is whether you are going to have a process that looks reasonably good commercially. . . . The number of processes is virtually infinite. We could have 50 to 75 processes that we could continue to put a little more money into each year.

"It's not going to solve the national problem, but it's going to keep a lot of research and development types happy."[14]

That is exactly what has happened. The government has given away billions of dollars to research programs which have done little or nothing to end our dependency on hostile suppliers or to end our rising inflation. For the bureaucracy this has meant more and more jobs. For the people of America it has meant higher and higher prices for food and other essentials and more and more suffering. Even the proposed cuts in synthetic fuels projects are not likely to solve the problem. President Reagan has not proposed to eliminate the subsidies for six new pilot projects. He has only proposed to eliminate the *direct* subsidies. Actually he is transferring authority to fund the pilot projects to the federally funded Synthetic Fuels Corporation. In addition, many of President Ronald Reagan's key advisers are as committed to the endless research as Carter's were. In fact, William J. Casey, the man who led Reagan's transition team, is also founder and director of a consulting firm that specializes in gaining huge government-funded energy-research contracts.

Meanwhile, the government can continue pointing to the massive amounts of money being spent on research and claim that a concrete effort to solve the energy problem is being made. Each year for forty years energy officials requested aid and each year Congress appropriated money to carry out more and more research without ever seriously questioning how the money was actually being spent or discussing the fact that the process already worked.

The same has been true for shale oil. Actually, shale oil is neither shale nor oil, it is a variety of limestone containing kerogen, a solid fossil fuel. The

companies are now conducting studies on how to
heat the host rock to 900°F in order to vaporize and
extract the kerogen. But again, the technology is
there. Again, for more than fifty years the oil
companies have been claiming that prices must go a
"bit" higher before they begin to produce shale oil.

In this case, too, it is more profitable for the
suppliers to accept big government research grants
and conduct meaningless studies. Back in 1971 the
oil companies were successful in setting up a
government corporation to develop oil shale and to
build plants, yet they still have not built a single
plant. This, despite the fact that for more than fifty
years they have known that the nation's oil shale
reserves are second only to coal. Twenty-two times
the nation's proved reserves of oil are considered
recoverable with current technology.

The recovery of only one-third of those reserves
would yield eight times the total known reserves of
Saudi Arabia.[15]

Obviously, building the plants and getting at
these reserves take time, and money, and it takes real
effort. The deliberate procrastination that has
replaced that effort has left the United States and its
food supply literally at the mercy of the OPEC
nations.

In effect, the huge oil companies are collabo-
rating against the American people. They are
refusing to produce until they extract the highest
possible profits from existing in-ground supplies.

The practical impact of this has driven energy—
and consequently food—costs so high that a lot of
people are already overwhelmed. Many must choose
between food and heat. In some areas there are
government-sponsored programs for fuel assistance
which are intended to reduce the suffering that the

same government's energy policies have created. People with very low incomes can call and see if they qualify. This, in itself, is demeaning to many men and women who are accustomed to managing on their own. It means going to a welfare office and sitting there for two or three hours just to fill out an application. Some people in their seventies and eighties simply don't have the physical strength or mental agility to do that. Those who do quickly find that there are many conditions attached. The fuel bill has to be in their name. For widows, if it is in their husband's name, they can forget it. They have to bring their personal identification, their Social Security number, their old fuel bills, and their proof of need. If they are lucky, they may be told that they will be given a credit on fuel of up to three hundred dollars. That sounds wonderful except before long it becomes clear to them that they must have three hundred dollars to buy the oil and then apply for a rebate. If they call the oil company and say they are cold and have run out of oil and qualify for fuel assistance, the company will say, "Is this going to be cash?" Unless they are established customers and the company knows they have money in the bank, it will not accept a check.

One woman I met who had an income from Social Security of $246.10 a month explained that she had heat from time to time but had decided, as people who want to survive must ultimately decide, that she needed food more. She told me that whenever she managed to save a hundred dollars in cash she would call the oil company and ask to have oil delivered. Every time she received oil she was charged an additional twenty-dollars service fee because the deliveryman had to start her furnace up again. She ran out of fuel three times in two months.

Even people who own their homes are often unable to keep them in good repair without storm windows or storm doors, and their monthly fuel bills are sometimes more than the entire Social Security check. Some people try to live in one room and turn the heat off in all the others. That way, they hope to keep warm and also fed.

In some cities if people run out of oil and have no money they can call a home heating oil emergency phone number. One woman in Philadelphia told me she had a broken oil burner and no money for repairing it. She called the emergency number but no one had any idea what she could do. There were no facilities for anything like that. "We can give you a couple days supply of oil," she was informed, "but if your burner is broken we can't help you. That's your problem." That woman was lucky. She persuaded a grandson-in-law to take a bank loan so that the heater could be repaired. She could then apply for assistance to put fuel in the heater. In March 1981 President Reagan proposed that this program too be scrapped. A woman I came to know in Boston who never had fuel aid confided in me, "I had to make a choice between food and heat. There just wasn't enough money for both so I lived without heat all winter. My one blanket didn't keep me warm and I slept in my hat and coat and mittens—covered with piles of newspapers."

A seventy-six-year-old heart patient with high blood pressure who lives in Philadelphia is still maintaining a coal heater because coal is "a little cheaper." As it is she can just barely afford the coal and have something left over for food. So several times a day she goes up and down the cellar steps and shovels the coal. "I may have a heart attack," she shrugged, "but at least I won't freeze or starve."

The truth is that even coal will not be "a little cheaper" for long. The oil industry is now accumulating large coal reserves in preparation for the time when the profits promise to be high enough for them to begin turning that coal into synthetic fuel. All twelve of the largest oil companies mine coal. Exxon now owns twelve times as much coal as oil, Mobil owns seventeen times as much coal as oil, and the Phillips Petroleum Company owns sixty-one times as much coal as oil. In addition, seven of the twelve biggest oil companies have an interest in every current and potential energy resource from natural gas to geothermal facilities. The companies are buying the power to control, for their own economic advantage, the pace and the price of *every* form of energy in America and the time that it is made available.

According to statistics compiled by the *Philadelphia Inquirer*, these companies have reserves vast enough to meet all of America's energy needs for more than eight hundred years without importing a single drop of foreign oil and without using nuclear energy.

Yet, instead of supplying this country with the fuel it so badly needs, all twelve of the largest companies are sitting on those reserves, waiting for the world price of oil to rise still higher. In the meantime, they continue conducting "research."

All twelve of the largest companies are expected to receive federal contracts which will add up to $2 billion by 1983 to finance more "research" into everything from solar energy to geothermal energy. All twelve of those companies are going to keep our energy costs as high as they can despite the human cost to millions of Americans.

Both food and fuel will become far more
expensive than they are now because every phase of
agriculture from the petroleum-based fertilizer to the
machines that harvest the crops and the trucks that
distribute the food depend on fuel. It really amounts
to this: The soaring cost of fuel is, to a large extent,
responsible for the rising cost of food. Decontrolling
the price of oil has brought more massive increases.
Yet, when the American people go to the supermarket
or to the gas pumps and stand helpless, amazed at
the changes, they seldom realize that they are
victims not only of the OPEC nations but of the
American oil companies and the American government. The effects of this system are pervasive and
they are far-reaching. Not only has the refusal to
develop our resources at reasonable prices made us
dangerously dependent on OPEC, it has also resulted
in the decline of the nation and the most massive
transfer of wealth in history.

In 1980 America spent $80 billion on imported
petroleum. The most direct consequences for the
American people are the higher costs of fuel and
food, but the consequences for the nation are an
enormous loss of money, power, and status. In 1971
America was the wealthiest nation in the world.
Now, according to World Bank statistics, it has
plunged not to second or third or fourth place but to
ninth place as measured by per capita gross national
product.

In a very direct way the government of the
United States is responsible for that decline. It is also
responsible for the soaring energy costs and for
placing its citizens in a position that leaves their food
production system at the mercy of unstable foreign
suppliers and greedy American companies. But four
successive administrations have done *nothing* to

prevent the accumulation or the abuse of power. Instead, Washington has encouraged it by failing to apply the same antitrust standards to the oil industry that it has applied to other industries.

In 1971 the Justice Department pledged to "scrutinize the oil industries acquisition of other fuel sources." Yet today, the oil companies own billions of tons of coal reserves, they own solar energy companies and geothermal companies, and have expanded their interests in nuclear energy. Despite this, the Justice Department claims that it has not detected *any* antitrust problems.[16]

Four successive administrations have failed to balance the interests of the majority of its citizens against the private interests of the energy corporations. They have aided and abetted a new breed of corporation which, with unmatched control and money, now determines how much of any kind of fuel will be made available. Since fuel effects the price and availability of food, they are also determining, only slightly less directly, how much of any kind of food will be available to the American people and at what price.

The twelve leading oil companies also own major uranium reserves, and they are responsible for hazards associated with mining of uranium that have already directly affected the food supply. These hazards occur outside of the big plants on land that is inhabited by people who have no voice at all in the profit-making interests of the large energy corporations. Their suffering, hunger, and death do not get newspaper coverage. Most of the American public does not know that the mining and milling of uranium for the production of nuclear energy has already killed crops, permanently destroyed cropland, and contaminated animals that provide food. Nor do many people know that the radiation released during that process enters the food chain and can affect people living hundreds of miles away.

Many government officials do know what is happening and what has been done and not done, but they seem to be working to suppress the long-range impact, at least until the land has been stripped and the big profits have been made.

7 Nuclear Power and Hunger

Uranium mining and milling are currently the most significant sources of radiation exposure to the public from the entire uranium fuel cycle, far surpassing other stages of the fuel cycle, such as nuclear power reactors or high-level radioactive waste disposal.
—The Nuclear Regulatory Commission

Fifteen years ago I visited an area high in the mountains of New Mexico. Wild flowers bloomed in abundance and sagebrush was mixed with small piñon and juniper trees. Deer, antelope, squirrels and rabbits darted among white yucca blossoms and red and yellow cactus blooms. From the road below I could see children in brightly colored clothing climbing on red and white sandstone mesas or peering out from behind rocks sculpted by wind, rain, and water.

At that time, almost every family raised all of its own food, in fields and gardens. Some of the food was sold in the nearby cities. Squash, corn, melons, beans, wheat, and oats grew in the ditch-irrigated farms and were the mainstay of life. The wealthier families slaughtered a sheep or goat nearly every week throughout the year, and even the poorest families always had food and could eat wild seeds for cereal and use the fruits of several species of cactus to make confections. Lamb, sheep, and butchered meat that was sold and shipped over long distances provided much of the income. Most of the shepherding was done by the children, who kept the flocks near home and brought them back to the same corral each night. Often they sang songs as they watched the animals graze. The life of these people hadn't changed for over a century.

I returned in 1979 and found that everything had changed. The grass would not grow. The sheep that had grazed on the grass had begun to starve and die. The horses suddenly fell ill, became bloated, and sometimes, within hours, they too were dead. The corn became short and stunted; its kernels turned red. The squirrels and rabbits and deer could no longer be found. Many of the streams had dried up and disappeared. Others had turned black and the children who played in them developed strange sores. The people who admitted that their animals had mysteriously died could not sell them for meat. They had no way to get money or food. Many were hungry, but they were afraid to eat the carcasses of the dead animals that lay rotting in the sun.

I sat inside a tiny gray hut with a wise old Navaho woman, who held out her hand to me and explained it this way. "My family doesn't have any food except for a few potatoes. When we had sheep we got mutton and cheese and milk and butter. Now we have nothing. In their rush for nuclear energy the big companies have left us without electricity. In their search for water they have made our wells run dry. In their effort to make money quickly they have left us starving. The land is rich with uranium but the people grow poorer. Soon this carelessness and greed will be felt everywhere."

She did not know that many Americans already felt the carelessness and greed she spoke of or that our own food supply had already been affected by the same energy companies. She knew only that her land was destroyed, that her agriculture—a subsistence agriculture but one which fed her and her children and her neighbors' children—had died along with the land. The ability to produce, grow and sell food had been lost. Land which was never rich but that, with care, had stood firm for centuries, had now grown poor and barren.

The people who lived on that land and farmed it had believed, as American farmers believed, that if they worked hard they would always have food to eat. Suddenly they found that they did not.

When I left that Navaho woman I did some research and found that the first uranium mines had opened during the 1950s in nearby Redrock. For a short time, everything had appeared normal. Then the land and the animals began to die. Some years later the miners themselves grew sick and many of them died from a strange, invincible small-cell carcinoma caused by chronic radiation exposure. The full effect of early mining in Redrock probably won't be known for another decade, but according to Dr. Gerald Bunker, a physician who studied the issue extensively, the risk of lung cancer alone was increased at least eighty-five fold.

"It is not just our land that has died or our food that won't grow," one woman explained; "each year a few more of our men die. Mostly it's just the women of us who are left with our children, and now some of the women and even the children have begun to cough and spit up blood."

The mines in Redrock closed in 1969 after the rich deposits of uranium ore had been depleted. But even now rain causes water from the mines to seep out and children playing in the streams have developed skin sores.

The Redrock Mines were run by Kerr-McGee, the Oklahoma-based coal, gas, and uranium giant—the same company that recently lost and then appealed a $10.5-million lawsuit that centered around the case of Karen Silkwood, a lab technician in a plant producing fuel rods for nuclear reactors. Karen Silkwood died mysteriously while driving to meet a *New York Times* reporter in an effort to document her charges that officials at the installation had knowingly exposed their employees to lethal doses of plutonium.

Now Kerr-McGee and approximately fifteen other energy companies seeking uranium have converged on Crownpoint, a tiny Navaho community in northern New Mexico. The companies have begun to drill test holes and construct mines. They claim that they have improved their techniques and that the problems that occurred in Redrock will not occur here, but the land and the animals in Crownpoint are dying already.

The men, women, and children who once herded the sheep and farmed the land now wander aim-

lessly, surveying the destruction. In many ways
Crownpoint is subject to the same abuse from the
energy companies that Redrock was. So is every
other American community where uranium is being
mined. Crownpoint is probably luckier than most,
because in Crownpoint there is group resistance
organized by a Navaho woman who left the reservation as a child, learned the white man's ways, and
then returned to protect her people.

When Elsie Peshlakai was seven, Mormon mis-
sionaries came to the reservation. They told her
about a grammar school she could go to in Utah, and
they said she would have parents there. She felt she
had to go because it was the only way she would
learn. She filled out the application but didn't tell
anyone because she knew her parents would not give
her permission. The day the bus came she climbed
on, her mother was away washing clothes. She rode
all night. The next day she met her foster mother. "I
remember when she gave me a bath," Elsie recalled,
"she said she had never seen skin this dark and felt
like she should keep scrubbing. I was scared but I
didn't cry. Then three and a half weeks later I went
up to the top of the lava rocks and I cried and cried.
Whenever we prayed I would pray to myself silently
in Navaho and promise myself that no one would
ever take the place of my own mother and father. I
always knew that after I became educated I would go
home and help my people."

After attending grammar school, high school,
and Brigham Young University, Elsie did return
home to Crownpoint. When she got there she found
that the Mobil Corporation had also arrived. The
miners had already made more than three thousand
test borings on the reservation where her family

lived. Her parents could no longer herd sheep on the land, and their crops had stopped growing. A mine was planned two hundred feet from their home. People told Elsie that they had heard rumors about a place called Redrock where the drillers had come and gone, where no food would grow and where everyone who worked in the mines had died or was dying. Then Elsie, who had studied chemistry and biology, began to go from home to home, talking to the Navahos about radiation.

Many of the families isolated from each other by the harsh land and the mesas had already begun to wonder separately why the corn was a quarter of its usual size and why the kernels were red. They wondered why the streams had gone dry and why the sheep that seemed well one day would lie flat, become bloated, and die within hours. Nor did they know what recourse they had when their sheep drowned in the claylike bentonite that the corporations used to fill the holes, or when a child of twelve was found dead of suffocation, in one of the ponds filled with bentonite. As Elsie Peshlakai traveled and explained what was happening, she also learned that many people had never given the large energy companies permission for their drilling rigs and miners.

It was ten degrees below zero when I sat beside Elsie Peshlakai in her blue, four-wheel drive pickup truck. We were going to see an old Navaho woman whose land had recently been confiscated. As we approached the entrance to the woman's allotment, we saw a large sign reading PRIVATE ROAD, MOBIL CONTRACTS, KEEP OUT. Ignoring the sign, we traveled up the long dirt road past hundreds of white stakes which marked the holes that had been drilled.

"As you can see, there is nothing growing out here anymore. The drilling and the bentonite have killed all of the crops," Elsie said as we approached a tiny gray hut with a red roof. Inside, I saw Ha-nah-bah Charley, wearing a brightly colored yellow skirt and a blue flowered blouse: long gray-black hair framed her face which was chiseled like leather stretched over bare bone. She greeted me softly in Navaho and smiled. I looked around at the kitchen—no sink or refrigerator, just an old table and a couple of chairs covered with torn plastic. Above her bed, on the walls once painted pink but now faded and cracked, I noticed a portrait of Christ with outstretched arms, leading a flock of sheep.

"My sheep are dead, I have no food," the woman said quietly in Navaho. "There are three large mud pits, each the size of this house. Some drowned in the mud, the others died one right after the other like they were poisoned."

"How many animals have died altogether?" I asked.

"Three calves, sixteen sheep, eleven goats, four horses," came the reply. "Now there is not enough food for the family because so many animals are dead. A white man from the Bureau of Indian Affairs came out to look at the dead sheep and said the deaths were probably caused by contaminated water since the wells Mobil dug have a runoff that goes right into the animals' stock pond."

"Why did you let them come here?" I asked.

When Elsie repeated the question, the old woman began to speak rapidly, gesturing with her hands, protesting. Elsie translated. "I didn't *let* them come. One day a white man carrying papers arrived with an Indian and said, 'Mother, because all is well with you and you use your land well, and you have no problems with your neighbors or your allotment, we want you to put your thumbprint right here on this piece of paper.' Trusting them, I agreed."

She pressed her thumb on the paper, not realizing that it was actually a contract that gave the Mobil Corporation access to 160 acres of some of the most energy-rich land in America. Her land.

"Later, I went to the Bureau of Indian Affairs office," Ha-nah-bah said, "and I told them what had happened and that my crops would no longer grow. They just looked me straight in the eye and said, 'Don't complain to us. It's your fault. You signed the paper.' " Suddenly the old woman looked up at me, worried. "Where are you from and why are you writing?" she asked.

Elsie explained that I had come from a place far away, near the White House, to write about the problem.

"Oh," she answered approvingly, "I don't know what happens in Washington, or how people live, but if more people know about it, Mobil and the other companies will not be able to lie to us."

When it was time to leave she asked if she could have some of the paper I was writing on. I gave her a yellow legal pad. She took the pen and put it to the paper and said, "If I'm not too old, I want to learn how to write."

"Would that help you to solve these difficulties?" I asked.

She smiled thoughtfully, then nodded her head and answered, "Yes, if I could read and write like you, I would have food today. Mobil and the Bureau of Indian Affairs would not be able to lie to me and get away with it."

"I feel with them. I am a Navaho." Ed Plummer, the middle-aged, heavyset director of the Bureau of

148

Indian Affairs for Crownpoint, New Mexico, told me later as he sat behind a large mahogany desk. "I grew up with them. The almighty dollar and the big oil companies have destroyed the land and the food. We might do reclaiming of the land, but what good is it if we have ruined the water? Right now we have contaminated water running down the creek from the United Nuclear Corporation. We could move these people to the cities, but Indians don't do well in the cities, they don't live that way. The land is where they have their ties."

I knew that he was right about that. I had seen what happened when Indians were moved to the cities after their land was destroyed. Chicago was the first relocation city that the Bureau had set up for Indians. I visited there in the spring of 1976.

The Indians in Chicago who had been taken off the land did not have traditional skills and 80 percent were out of work. Their nutrition was so poor that many of the children were growing up deformed. They had no school breakfast programs, no hot lunches for senior citizens, and no home-delivered meals.

There was only one program for Indians in uptown Chicago. Funded by the U.S. Department of Health, Education and Welfare, it was designed to be a crisis intervention center for alcoholic Indians, but because there were so many more hungry Indians than alcoholic ones, the crisis center actually looked more like a soup kitchen.

A sign with the word Bu-sho-ne-gee, which means "Welcome, friend" in Chippewa, hung on the blue wall. Three long tables filled the converted store. Behind the counter there was an open kitchen where soup was kept warm in a large pot. Most of the people who ate at Bu-sho-ne-gee were getting all of their food there.

The funding is for alcoholics, so we can't let the kids stay too long, Gerald Litman, the psychiatric social worker who ran the place, had explained, but the fact is that no one else provides food for these kids or their mothers.

An old Indian woman walked in, her hair in braids. She was very poor and had little food. Her husband had just died. No one knew exactly why he had died; there had been some speculation about malnutrition but the woman didn't want to talk about it. Her main concern was to get him buried back on the reservation. She had been working unsuccessfully all day to collect enough money to take his body home. Toward evening her mouth began to move noiselessly as if in prayer and her feet began to tap the floor. "Maybe we could put the body in my station wagon and you could get enough money to pay for the gas," someone had suggested as a last resort. But the woman didn't answer or even acknowledge the offer. Her eyes were staring straight ahead and there were tears in them.

After I left the center I bought a pizza for dinner and sat alone in my rented car. I couldn't eat, so I started the car and drove to a nearby housing project to meet Annie BosJarlait, an American Indian who lived there with her daughter and four other Indian children. I had been told that the makeshift family usually survived on soup, white rice, and fried bread made of flour, baking powder, and salt.

But the night I visited the BosJarlait house on North Kenmore there was a sense of lethargy and despair, which suggested that things were worse than usual. The $210 welfare check was a month late.

Dirty laundry was piled in a corner because there was not enough money for the Laundromat. A $209 oil bill, covering several months, lay on the broken living room table. The welfare caseworker had failed to return Annie's calls.

"This has been going on for a long time," she explained. "Now the baby is anemic and we have no money for iron."

I looked at the three boys and two girls sitting on the couch, silently eating popcorn. "What do you do when you run out of food?" I asked.

She laughed, embarrassed. "I serve the children popcorn," she answered, and then lowered her head.

"I had pizza for dinner tonight," I said, "and I couldn't finish it. Most of it is outside in the car." I spoke quickly, afraid that they might be offended.

"Pizza!" the children shouted in unison, and it sounded like a cry of joy.

"Pizza!" the mother echoed.

"Come on," I said, and we ran out in the rain to the car.

Now, three years after that experience, I turned to the Navaho director of the Crownpoint Bureau of Indian Affairs and asked, "Isn't it difficult for you as an Indian to stand by and see the land destroyed and your people driven into the cities where they are so poor and so hungry?" When he didn't respond, I continued pressing him: "You know as well as I do what happens when they are driven off the land."

Suddenly he hardened. "I've been here for eleven years. I'm satisfied, I'm happy as hell. They have all these options." He looked at his watch. "I have to be going," he said. "Please remember that I represent the Secretary of the Interior. I am charged by him with all of these responsibilities. I am following the regulations. I am taking care of everything."

Actually most Bureau of Indian Affairs' administrators are not following the regulations. Sara McCray, a dark-eyed, highly spirited, middle-aged Navaho woman, who still lives on the reservation, explained that back in 1974 two people came to her. One was from the Bureau, the other was from a large oil company. They said they wanted to lease one acre of her land for a hundred dollars for one year. Wanting to be cooperative, she agreed. Then the oil company began to bring in equipment, placing it over the entire 160-acre allotment. Sometime later, the company man returned to her house with a Navaho representative, this time saying they wanted to put in one little light bulb because they had come across some bedrock. "Please, please sign it," said the Indian man, speaking in Navaho. Because he was a Navaho she trusted him. Again she agreed and signed her name to a form he presented. After that the company put power lines all over her land.

Three or four months later, a white man with a big beard came and said they had discovered uranium on her land and they wanted her to sign her name. This time she said no. She told him that she was poor and she was humble, but she was also tired of being tricked and lied to. This time before I sign, she said, I want you to drill for water so that we can have water to drink and water for our livestock. He said, "Yes, we will do that for you if you will sign your name." She said, "No, I want it done first then I will sign my name." He just laughed, rolled up his contract, and left.

Two months later he returned again and asked her if she had thought about it. She said, "Yes, but have you thought about making me the well?" He said, "No, we don't do that. That will cost you a lot of money." She said, "Then I'll never sign my name. You've lied to me again and again. I'm going to find out what is at the bottom of this. I'm sure there's a lawyer who will help me. I hear there's a meeting in Crownpoint and I'm going to go."

Sara McCray went to that meeting in July 1978. It was there that she met Elsie Peshlakai and learned how wise she was to have refused to sign the papers.

She also met Shirley Roper, a young Navaho woman who, like Elsie, left home as a young child to live with the Mormons and become educated. When Shirley returned with a B.A. degree and two years of postgraduate training in clinical psychology, she found hundreds of holes drilled in her land.

"Slowly I am learning that life in America is a treacherous game," Shirley said. "I believe that this kind of progress signals inevitable destruction. It's total upheaval. It's human sacrifice. Talk about Indian givers. First they throw us on this land and then they want to take it back. They gave it to us because they thought it was no good. Now they say it is their last resource for nuclear energy; uranium from our land is filling the cities with lights and we still have no electricity. We are making machines run that bring food to others—yet we have no machines and the food we grow has been destroyed. They are using uranium from our land to create weapons for defense. What are they going to defend? A radioactive field where everyone is starving or has cancer? It's hard to know who's more naive, the Navahos who signed the papers or the oil companies who think only of money."

For Shirley's mother, Mae Roper, the pain is greater. She was so timid in front of white men that when they asked her to sign a paper giving up her land she did. Now she deeply regrets it. "We are told that the land we own is worth millions," she explained. "If that is true, then we should be millionaires. Yet we have nothing, not even food. I have only got a few more years to live, but my children and grandchildren will hold me responsible for opening up the mine and ruining the land. I signed the paper and I fear that my Maker will send me off to hell. I thought maybe we could put up a church on the mesa to ask God to forgive us for signing and forgive the white men for what they are doing."

Then she turned to Elsie who was translating this from Navaho and said, "No more signatures, Elsie; you must go into the homes and tell them. You are the only one who could. Our whole way of dealing with life has been to accept and accept."

"Yes," Elsie said, "even now our own people who don't look beyond today think we are taking away jobs. They forget how quickly all the uranium will be used up, and how the companies will move on until there is nowhere left to move. They forget that our people will begin to die of cancer and that food will be destroyed. Sometimes I wonder what the white men will do after they have destroyed our land and have taken everything left in the earth. I wonder if they will begin to die slowly of hunger and disease as they are causing us to die. We are starting to ask questions. We are starting to talk here on the reservation. Yes, I have to go into the homes and get them to trust me."

Then Elsie put her hand on Mae Roper's shoulder and said in Navaho, "No more signatures—it's survival now."

Elsie Peshlakai may be able to prevent further

uranium-mining expansion in Crownpoint, New Mexico, but the dangers to food, land, crops, and people are being echoed all over America.

David Dreesen, a scientist at the Los Alamos Scientific Laboratory, wrote in a departmental newsletter, "Perhaps the solution to the radon [radiation] problem is to zone the land in uranium mining and milling districts so as to forbid human habitation."

But even that won't contain the contamination. Radioactive materials can affect people who do not live in the area because they are suspended in the atmosphere and dispersed over many hundreds of acres by wind, erosion, rain, and snow. Infiltration into ponds, streams, and drinking water is also common.

If the radioactivity enters the food chain, people eating the food will not be safe. The radioactive materials are reabsorbed into the earth through rain and snow. If they seep into the root systems of the vegetation and crops that have not been destroyed, animals grazing on the contaminated vegetation and people eating the food or the animals could ultimately absorb their radiation.

As long as the major energy companies are allowed to continue carelessly mining uranium while postponing the production of other available and less dangerous forms of energy, land loss, crop destruction, and hunger will not remain localized. They will become widespread and pervade all aspects of life in America.

8   Destroying the Land

We are on a collision course with disaster. Our water supplies are being reduced, we have whole watersheds where the groundwater reserves are being depleted and we have mined our soil. In fact the erosion of America's farmland today is probably at a record rate. This simply cannot go on.
      —Bob S. Bergland, Secretary of Agriculture
      Face the Nation, CBS Television Network,
      November 26, 1978

In order to prevent hunger from increasing and from spreading across this country, America must have two basic and essential resources—energy and land.

The energy must be accessible, reasonably priced, reasonably safe, and uninterrupted in supply so that farmers can afford to sell their crops for moderate prices and count on harvesting them when they need to. The land must be plentiful and well cared for so that it can endure and produce.

America was blessed with wonderful natural abundance. We have enough energy for all of our needs, except that the energy is being hoarded by huge companies and withheld from the people. We also have or had enough rich, fertile, life-giving land, except that now that land is being destroyed.

In many ways, then, Crownpoint, New Mexico, is a microcosm of America. The Navaho woman who told me that Americans will do to themselves what they have done to her people was right. In Crownpoint the careless search for uranium by the same companies who are withholding other available energy sources destroyed the land and the ability to produce food.

In much of the rest of America farmers are also faced with the destruction of their land. Often it is even more pointless and its effect will be even more far reaching, because if this country suffers serious food shortages, so will the rest of the world.

Since World War II the United States has become a dominant world food supplier. Of the 115 countries for which statistics are available, all but a few count on the United States for food.[17]

The world population is expected to increase and to increase greatly. About ten years from now, there are likely to be five billion people on this earth and by the year 2000 we can expect six or seven billion people. Many of those people will be depending on America for food. Poor countries will need three times the level of food assistance they are now receiving. And they will have difficulty paying for the food because of the rising cost of oil.[18] In August 1980, a U.S. presidential panel released an eight-hundred-page, three-year study which predicted that even wealthy nations would only have sufficient oil through 1990 and that the number of malnourished people in the world would rise to 1.3 billion by the year 2000.[19]

Even if the energy companies made sufficient fuel available as soon as they could, America's agricultural system would still have to expand greatly in order to maintain our current levels of support, and emergency aid. If our present policies continue, we will not be able to expand at all or even maintain our present levels of productivity because we will not have enough land left on which to expand. In addition, we are treating the land we have so badly that it no longer yields what it once did.

According to the Department of Agriculture, grain yields peaked in 1972 and have continued to drop each year since then. In 1973 then Secretary of State Henry Kissinger warned the United Nations Emergency Food Conference that "The world has come to depend on a few exporting countries, particularly the United States, to maintain the necessary reserves but reserves in America no longer exist, despite the fact that the United States has removed virtually all restrictions on production and farmers have made an all-out effort to maximize output." Just one year earlier, in 1972, there had still been enough extra land so that farmers had been paid $3.6 billion to hold it out of production. At that time, one acre of prime land was kept out for every four and one-half acres planted. Today there is no extra prime farmland. It has all been destroyed. Food

158

production ultimately comes back to the need for land, fertile land, prime land. We can't survive without it, yet all those rich American farm reserves are now gone. Increasing production on the seventy-five million acres of marginal land that is still left in America would require three times the amount of energy that we now use to drain, grade, and irrigate prime land. America has destroyed thirty million acres of farmland in ten years. At that rate, even without an energy crisis, the country's ability to feed itself and a growing world population could be gone by the year 2000. Experts in agricultural economy warn that food supplies could be drastically reduced and prices could skyrocket by the end of the decade if the trend continues.[20] And, so far, it *is* continuing. Having run out of unused prime land, this nation has actually, and almost unbelievably, begun to destroy its own best, currently planted land. Four square miles of rich, productive, crop yielding farmland are now destroyed each day.

The importance of this farmland, the growing need to save what is left to grow food that can support human life, and the value of the skilled, hardworking, productive farmer have still not been understood by policymakers. Instead, all over this country our farmers are treated as if they were squatters on the land they have owned and cared for all of their lives, and our limited supply of prime, life-yielding cropland is treated as if it were literally an endless reservoir.

The destruction of the Valley of the Little Tennessee provides an example of the kind of immediate personal suffering and long-term national damage that is so typical. This farmland was unsurpassed for the depth of its topsoil, for its richness, its history, and its beauty. It had long been known for the fine productivity of its soil. Yet, in December 1978, thirty-eight thousand acres were needlessly flooded by the combined official orders of Congress, the Tennessee Valley Authority, and the President of the United States. Some of the best and most productive of that farmland belonged to Ben Richie, a man who loved his land and fought hard to keep it.

I first met Ben Richie at the crossroads just past the floodgates of the Tellico Dam Project. He was waiting in his old pickup truck when I arrived with Boon Dougherty, his attorney. We were an hour late, but when Ben Richie saw us he just smiled—he was used to waiting. He had waited ten years for a final government decision, holding onto his land, planting it, harvesting it, tending it, and hoping, constantly hoping, that Congress and the Tennessee Valley Authority would reverse their position and decide not to flood the land and build the proposed dam and industrial park. Even after they handed him a condemnation notice and sent him a check and seized the land, Mr. Richie kept hoping; he politely returned the check, insisted on paying his taxes, and went right on planting the land.

Then the TVA sent bulldozers that began to circle endlessly in front of his old farmhouse. Soon afterward the power company and telephone company yielded to TVA pressure and threatened to cut off service. But Ben Richie and his wife decided that since they had lived half of their lives without phones or electricity, they could do it again. They didn't scare easily.

Now I drove behind Ben Richie's truck and followed him down a long dirt driveway that led to a modest white farmhouse a mile from where his own home had been torn down and buried. He climbed out of the truck, smiled again, and held out a calloused hand to greet me. After we shook hands he turned to the left, raised his head high, squinted, and looked up the road toward his place. He didn't have to tell me that no matter what was done it would always be his place; something in his eyes made the statement.

The Richie family was living temporarily in a neighbor's house, like fugitives, close enough so that they could watch over the land and, one last time, harvest the crops that had not been flooded.

Ben Richie led me in. His wife Jean, a small, bright-eyed, cheerful lady, and her three pretty school-teacher daughters greeted me. I sat down in the rocking chair; the family sat across from me lined up on an old sofa covered with a spread. Everyone was dressed in flannel shirts and dungarees and work shoes. As they sat there next to the old stove, I told them that they looked like a classic photograph of the typical American farm family. "That's what we were," Jean Richie responded warmly, "before we became the Tellico boat people." Then she laughed, but it was the kind of joke that hurt.

Actually, the notion of flooding the farmland to create a dam on the Little Tennessee River first emerged in Congress in 1936 but nothing was done until June 1942 when funds were made available. Then, in October of that year, the War Production Board decided that because of war priorities the project should be shelved and the whole idea was dropped. By the time the proposal was reopened it was 1963 and the estimated cost had risen from $10.7 million to $41 million.

Strenuous opposition by landowners and the Tennessee Valley State Planning Commission developed immediately, forcing Congress to hold hearings to discuss the economic and environmental concerns and possible benefits. At first Congress appeared to favor the opposition, but in 1966, in a surprise move, it approved the initial appropriation and in 1967, despite opposition, construction began. Each year additional funds were allocated and by 1975 the project was 75 percent complete. Its estimated cost had increased again—to $100 million.

All this time no one knew exactly *why* the dam was being built. The TVA called it "a means of improving the standard of living and quality of life of the region's people through the development of the region's natural resources."[21] Many disagreed. In December 1978 the *Los Angeles Times* called Tellico a "damn waste," and said its potential economic benefit to the region was nil. The *Philadelphia Inquirer* added that the dam was totally unjustified from a standpoint of economic benefits and that it would kill a great deal of valuable farmland for no useful purpose.

But TVA had acquired or condemned much of the best, most productive farmland in Blount, Loudon, and Monroe counties for this dam, and whether or not the project was of value, they had made up their minds to continue. Ultimately, the TVA won and American taxpayers paid more than $100 million to flood the richly productive farmland.

Here, word for word, is how Jean Richie described what it felt like to be driven off her land and out of her home by the TVA and the government.

One day in 1969 when two of my daughters were still in high school a man came; he knocked on the door and when I answered he told me he was going to appraise our whole property. I was just bowled over. My husband Ben was out in the fields sowing spring oats. I told the man we didn't want to sell, but that TVA could have, free of charge, the land they wanted to flood near the creek.

He went away and five years passed before anyone made contact with us again. Then in the spring of 1974 two fellows came. We told them the same thing, but this time they were more persistent. They came and came and came. When we wouldn't give in and agree to sell the entire farm, they began to threaten us. They brought in earth-moving equipment that made our whole house shake. They acted like they were going to tear the house down while we were inside it. Just collapse it right on our heads. They tried every way in the world to intimidate us. They even washed out our little bridge. Boy, they were some people, I tell you. But no matter what they did, we never agreed to sell our land. Then one day in amazement and horror we read in the newspaper that we had "passed title" of our one hundred and nineteen acres to the United States government. We rushed to the courthouse to claim our deed and found that it was no longer there. Shortly after that the federal marshals brought us the condemnation papers and a check.

The check was so much lower than the real value of the land that we couldn't begin to replace it with the money they paid. When we got those papers and that check, we felt so lost

and so defeated that we just closed our
front door and wept. To think that your
own government would do that to you.
It means that none of us are safe, we
can't even count on keeping what we
own. The government can come in any
time and claim and confiscate anyone's
private property. I equate TVA with the
government because they get their
funding from Congress and a lot of our
congressmen become rubber stamps for
what TVA proposes. There is no close
scrutiny in Congress. That's how these
things go through. In our case, even if
there had been a need to build a dam
they didn't have to tear our house down
to do it. The water for the dam didn't
even come near our house. Still, they
were determined to destroy it, so that
we could never come back and live in it
and farm our land again. They obtained
a writ of assistance from the federal
marshals, and told us that they would
"drag us out bodily" if we did not agree
to move. At that point we gave up and
agreed.

Actually Jean Richie and her family hadn't
really given up. They could never do that, but they
had figured out what they needed to do to reduce
their loss as much as possible. They had learned
quite a lot about the people they were dealing with.

We knew that if we refused they
would confiscate our machinery and
that it would become unavailable for

thirty days. We had a couple of fields of soybeans that would be flooded when they opened the gates, so how could we allow our machinery to be confiscated? We needed that machinery to get those beans out before they dropped the floodgates. We knew we had lost the struggle, but we were determined to salvage whatever we could.

When I came back the day they tore the house down, no one said a word to me; they acted like they didn't even see me. I know they did, but they kept pretending I wasn't there, even when I made these pictures. Here's a picture of our house. That's all underwater now. That was the view from our front porch. We could see the whole horizon. It was a good, strong, substantial house. It was about sixty-five years old. They started tearing it down in the morning. They worked all day at destroying it. Here's another view of the pile of rubble. That shows you how they tore down one of the barns. Here are the two barns piled up. I shook all over when I made these pictures. Here's our little chicken house.

The house was made out of pine and all of this lumber could have been used for something, for firewood at least. There were many people in the neighborhood who could have used it to keep warm or to build things. We could have used it ourselves. But they dug a hole and buried it right in what used to be our garden spot. They were determined to destroy everything, even the last remains.

Now TVA tells us that Coors Beer may build a factory on the part of our land that they didn't flood. They say that it will bring jobs to the area and prove that they were right to destroy the farmland. How are we going to feel if our farm is used to make Coors Beer? And where will they get the land to grow the grain to make the beer if they keep this kind of thing up? When they slam the farmers into the dirt, and flood their crops, and build factories on their land, that's when people are going to be hungry. Just think how many people could have been fed with the food we grew on our land. They aren't just hurting us, they are hurting America, only they don't know it yet.

Jean Richie didn't want to hurt anyone, not even the people from the TVA who had hurt her so badly. She paused for a few seconds after that long, emotional speech to collect herself, then she said she guessed it was lunchtime and told her daughters to go on into the kitchen and serve the soup and make the iced tea. After a few minutes they called us in and we sat around the old kitchen table, eating the fine homemade soup and talking about how the government was originally created to help the people and do what was in their interest and how hard it was to accept all this destruction when it served no purpose.

After lunch we piled into the Richies' old car and drove down a wide dirt road that had recently been cut straight through the deserted corn and bean fields to run alongside the flooded ground. The three daughters spoke excitedly, often at once. "They named this the Tellico Parkway," one of them said. "They call it a 'scenic road.' But the land and the crops and all of the scenery that was beautiful to us have been destroyed now." Then another pointed out of the window. "See the patch of brown right over there beyond those trees? That's where our house used to be. And over there is where our school was. You can tell by the fresh dirt. They destroyed everything in sight even if they didn't need to flood it." And again, pointing, "Here's where Daddy used to have his beans. There's nothing on the soil now to keep it from eroding. That topsoil will flow right down into the water."

Then Jean Richie silenced her daughters and picked up the story again, telling me that a whole village, a good, farming community, had been lost forever and for nothing.

> The church we always went to was right over there under that water. And those silos, sticking out of the water, were once part of a farm. They never even took the silos down.
>
> It was strange. Just before the land was flooded the archaeologists were out here desperately digging up the remains of the Indian civilization while TVA was enthusiastically burying ours. You know, someday in the future when people need food and can't get enough, I believe that they will come back to this flooded place and ask what happened to the land out here in the 1970s and I think they'll conclude

that the American people went off their
rockers.

She didn't want me to think they were bitter or
angry or hostile people and I knew that they weren't.
They were remarkably cheerful, but she went on to
explain:

> Except for the day they brought
> over the condemnation papers, we never
> sat down and grieved about it. All the
> threats just made us appreciate our
> place more than ever. Every morning
> when we went out we thought the birds
> sang prettier and the trees looked better
> and the land looked richer. Every day
> we just kept hoping. Right up to the
> very end we always believed that right
> would prevail, we really did. Even
> though we were fighting with the gov-
> ernment and we hated to fight, when we
> lay down at night we had a clear
> conscience. We knew we were right and
> that made us believe that we would win.

There was something else that had given the
Richies hope. Back in January 1976 their attorney
had filed the snail darter endangered species suit,
which contended that the building of the dam would
cause the elimination of the fish, and by April 1976
they had a trial. Ironically, many people who had not
responded to the critical loss of prime farmland or
the plight of the Richies and the other farmers whose
land was confiscated and whose homes were destroyed did respond to the concept that there was an
endangered species. They responded to the three-inch
snail darter with such vigor that the U.S. Sixth

Circuit Court issued an injunction enjoining any further activity with regard to the Tellico Project.

"TVA thought it was crazy to fuss about an endangered species," Jean Richie's oldest daughter told me. "The local press and a lot of others made it sound ridiculous. A three-inch fish versus a hundred-million-dollar dam. But I was glad that the court cared about *something*, even if they didn't care about us. I always felt, and I feel today, that there was something to it, that it was wrong for TVA to think that their creation was more important than God's creation and wrong that they wiped out God's creation with theirs."

The case went to the Supreme Court of the United States. In June 1978 the Supreme Court came back with a decision saying that it totally and permanently forbade the project. The TVA then turned the problem over to Congress. Jimmy Carter's people said that Carter was not going to authorize the project. But when the crunch came, a deal was made.

Here, according to plaintiff attorney Zig Potter, is how that deal was made.

> We were pressing hard for Carter to stand strong. We had thirty-five organizations pushing for a veto. We had a head count in both the House and the Senate to sustain the veto. The day before the deadline we heard that the congressional liaison, Frank Moore, had told the President that unless the dam was built he'd be cartooned with a killer rabbit on one side and a snail darter on the other and that Jimmy Carter had believed that.
>
> Carter left for New York to give a

speech on Tellico, still undecided about
what he would do. He had two speeches
with him. One that he would use if he
vetoed the proposal and another he'd
use if he did not. Then when he got on
the plane he signed the bill to flood the
land.

That same day, Carter telephoned
me and said he had done it for the good
of the nation. "After careful analysis
and soul searching," Carter said, "I determined to sign the bill. It was a close
decision but I think it was in the country's best interest." I said, "You don't
build strength by taking a position of
weakness, Mr. President." He said, "I
don't think it was weakness." I said,
"This is a big mistake." "I won't know
that for several years," he answered.
Subsequently the staff people told me
he had actually made a deal: he had
traded support for Tellico for the promise of votes he needed on the SALT
treaty.

I thanked him for calling and then
I said I guessed that there was nothing
more for us to talk about. "I wanted to
make the gesture because I know how
long you've worked on this," he answered. "It was not the gesture I've
worked for, President Carter," I said. I
was angry because I'd never walked on
topsoil that rich and that deep. I knew
we needed the land and that we would
need it even more in the future. Carter's
a nice man. He worked hard for the

right things. He agonized over them, but in this case he traded his friends and his own values for a decision that he thought was politically expedient.

TVA attorney Jim Burger saw things differently. He pointed out that $117 million had already been spent. He acknowledged that at least another $13 million would have to be spent and that a lot of people would be displaced, but he maintained that it was the right thing to do. Then Burger reminded me that TVA had made no recommendation to the Congress and that President Carter had independently signed that bill into law. "We were told, not asked," he added. "We merely carried out the policies of Congress and the TVA board. You must remember that no one thought about preserving land when TVA began to build these dams. It's too bad we didn't see what was coming."

Officially, TVA did see what was coming. In June 1978, a full year and a half *before* the Tellico Project was completed and the Richies and the other farmers were driven off the land, S. David Freeman, chairman of the board of the Tennessee Valley Authority, gave a speech to employees in which he said, "This loss of prime farmland is not trivial. It is important. Each acre of prime land that is lost requires that many acres of less productive and more erosive land be used to produce the same amount of food."

Freeman warned his staff that the world population was expected to double in the next twenty years and that the nation faced much greater expense and a much greater hazard from erosion. He told them that more and more of our prime farmland was being gobbled up by the developers and the fast-buck artists and that no one, at least no one in the

Tennessee Valley, was doing anything about it. He said that he was deeply concerned because, unless the country started taking some effective action to stop the current trend, Americans would wake up one day and see nothing but hamburger stands stretching from the Great Smoky Mountains to the Mississippi River. "Even worse," he warned, "there won't be enough pastures left to produce the hamburgers."

Later, speaking to the Subcommittee on Fisheries and Wildlife Conservation and the Environment for the U.S. House of Representatives, Freeman went further: He pointed out that it was not just the snail darter that had been discovered as an endangered species. The nation was beginning to discover that prime farmland was also an endangered species.[22]

After those speeches TVA's farm experts had provided Freeman and the rest of the board of TVA with a preliminary analysis of the benefits that this farmland could provide. It had shown that the total farm sales from the land had been $8.5 to $15 million a year. TVA experts also estimated that food production could generate farm-related business in the area of another $37 million each year. The difference between using the land for food production rather than flooding it would have been as great as $50 million a year and could also have created 2900 new farm-related jobs. When these figures were contrasted with the benefits of building the dam, it became clear that the farm value was far greater than the dam value. Despite that clear knowledge, and Freeman's speeches, the land was destroyed and the hardworking farmers who fought back were threatened, intimidated and finally left homeless.

Of course, the Tellico Dam with its loss of thirty-eight thousand acres will not, in itself, break the

American agricultural system or change the American life-style. Only those people who were displaced will have their lives changed forever by the destruction of this land. Even the estimated $138 million that will be spent for Tellico can be written off. But Tellico is a significant event in a long and ongoing history of land destruction which *will* break the American agricultural system if it is not stopped.

Almost before the ink had dried on Carter's seal of approval for completing the Tellico Dam, the TVA was attempting to proceed with construction of the Columbia Dam on the Duck River in Maury County, Tennessee. The Columbia Dam would result in agricultural losses of an additional $14 million annually. One out of every 18 acres of farmland in two counties would be lost at an estimated cost to the taxpayers of $153 million. Fifteen endangered species would be obliterated and 260 families would be displaced; 31,800 additional acres of American farmland would be lost to agriculture. That would bring the amount of land that the Tennessee Valley Authority alone had taken out of farm production to 1.1 million acres.

Experts at the U.S. Department of Agriculture are quietly studying the reports of their own computer studies, which indicate that "at the rate this country is destroying prime and unique farmlands the impact will be felt, in the form of reduced food supplies and higher prices, as early as the turn of the century." The computers show that five million acres of land, including one million acres of prime cropland, are being lost each year.

M. Rupert Cutler, assistant secretary of agriculture of the Conservation, Research, and Education Department in the Carter administration, calls the land destruction facts "unassailable and brutal. In one generation we have paved over land with concrete and asphalt the equivalent of the land area of several eastern states."[23]

The land in this country had always seemed so limitless, so indestructible, so powerful, and so bountiful that some Americans thought there would be enough no matter how much was destroyed. They also thought that the land would produce no matter how it was mistreated and plundered and abused by man's carelessness and greed. Now it seems that the permanent destruction of fine, rich, life-giving American farmland is only one of the land-related issues that threatens the amount of food this country will be able to produce.

Often the land that is not taken out of production is so badly treated and so mercilessly misused that an additional two hundred million acres has been ruined or almost destroyed by erosion of topsoil. Today erosion continues to remove soil much faster than it is being formed.[24] The topsoil now being lost to erosion will be formed again . . . at the rate of *one* inch each hundred years.

Soil cannot sustain a loss of more than five tons of topsoil an acre each year without damaging its ability to grow food. That is widely known and clearly understood, and yet in the United States the average loss to erosion in America's farmland is about twelve tons an acre each year. Soil losses of forty to fifty tons an acre each year are not uncommon. In extreme cases losses as high as sixty tons an acre have been recorded in the United States and allowed to continue.[25]

Soil erosion persists despite billions of dollars that are allocated, supposedly, to prevent it. According to the General Accounting Office, part of the problem is that the Department of Agriculture has not sought out the farmers who need the help. Instead, most of the funds provided for agricultural stabilization and conservation have actually been spent on short-term efforts to improve crop yields. This has occurred despite Agriculture's having been told by its own Department of Conservation, Research and Education that two-thirds of the cropland and pastureland in America badly needs additional protection against erosion.

When land loses its topsoil to erosion, it becomes unable to support crops. This in turn causes farmers to apply greater and greater pressure to the land they have left that is still productive, further damaging its topsoil. It also leads farmers to cultivate millions of acres of marginal land, which they are likely to farm carelessly and destroy quickly.

Nebraska is typical. Over eighteen thousand acres of Nebraska rangeland has recently been brought into crop production. According to Nebraska's Lower Loop Natural Resource District manager, Richard Beran, the soil, commonly known as valentine soil, is too light and too unstable to be cultivated without serious danger of wind erosion. Despite that, the rolling sand hills have been bought by absent corporate investors and it is now being farmed with massive irrigation systems.

Irrigation of the soil is not in itself bad, but in America, farmers are using irrigation to make land that shouldn't be farmed usable for a short time. The nature of the tiller is that he stays in one place and husbands the soil so that year after year the same ground will provide him with what he needs. Instead, American farmers are cultivating land that should only be used for grazing.

American farmers are repeating the Dust Bowl pattern. They have forgotten that on May 11, 1934,

350 million tons of Oklahoma's marginal topsoil was hit by a windstorm and that the soil actually exploded in huge clouds. They have forgotten that there was so much dust that ships three hundred miles out at sea were covered with it. Twelve million tons hit Chicago alone. In Washington, D.C., dust particles seeped in through closed windows and settled on congressional desks. It happened because farmers cultivated marginal land and stopped taking care of it. Just as they are doing now. After the disaster the government ordered the planting of millions of trees—greenbelts which would slow down the erosion from wind and protect the topsoil. The trees worked well for nearly forty years. But in 1973 when grain prices rose, Secretary of Agriculture Earl Butz ordered that the trees be cut down. "Plant fence row to fence row," he said. Within a year, fifty-one million acres of land had been taken out of the federally subsidized soil bank program and converted to cropland, without soil preparation or good conservation practices. Soil losses from fifty to two hundred tons per acre resulted.

Much of that land has been so badly damaged that now it cannot be used for anything, not even for grazing cattle. It will take twenty-five years to restore those greenbelts, to plant new trees and have them grow, and in many areas all the topsoil will be blown away by then.

Today America is cultivating millions of acres of marginal land and less than half of it is being farmed under good conservation practices. As a result, this country is losing in topsoil alone the equivalent of thirty 100-acre farms *each* day. That amounts to a yearly loss of one ton of topsoil for each person on earth.

America has already lost about one-third of its

farmland. If we continue at our present rate of destruction, another third will be lost in the next twelve to fifteen years. Right now an acre of land can just barely feed one person. Twenty years from now— with continued loss of land and increasing population—hunger in America will be extensive. Statistics indicate that three people then will be trying to eat from each acre that is left.[26]

All across this country, the land is losing its ability to produce. California has the largest food and fiber industry in America. In 1979, Governor Jerry Brown warned the state legislature that it would cost "hundreds of millions of dollars for California to deal with its advanced erosion problems," and if the state did not, he continued, "the same fate that confronted the civilization of Northern Africa and the Tigris and Euphrates will confront us here in California."

Brown wasn't just trying to scare the legislature. Experts were also pointing to the dangerous pattern, but no one could get the legislature to respond or the farmers to stop abusing the soil before all of its life-producing topsoil was gone. Soil, explained Dr. Priscilla Grew, director of the Department of Conservation for the State of California, is the very foundation of California's $14 billion annual agricultural and timber production program. If the best we can do is to "grow an inch of new topsoil in a hundred years, it is clear that our strategy should be to conserve the soil we already have. Wastage of our topsoil is as much erosion of our national capital as losing shavings off of gold bars in Fort Knox."

Dr. Grew is not a politician seeking votes or a person given to making alarming statements casually. She is a scientist, a geologist with her Ph.D.

from the University of California, a ten-year academic career, and seven research grants. When I
spoke with her, she had also just completed an intensive two-year investigation and inventory of California soils. That inventory had revealed critical
wind erosion, salinity, and drainage problems in
600,000 acres of California cropland in twenty
counties including 400,000 acres in the San Joaquin
Valley alone. Dr. Grew had pointed out to the
legislature that California appeared all too prom-
inently on the United Nations map of advancing
desertification. She had also explained that she
believed conditions would continue to grow worse
primarily because Americans had an awareness
problem. The urban people didn't know about the
land issues and the rural people felt that there was
nothing they could do about them.

When Dr. Grew became director of the California
Department of Conservation, there was absolutely no
state assistance for soil conservation. She spent two
full years telling people in government why they
needed a program. Then she proposed a five-year
plan with $20 million in grants and loans for
rehabilitation of California's croplands and range-
lands. The program was part of a larger plan to
restore natural resources.

Dr. Grew had hoped to deal with 9 million acres
damaged by erosion, 1.8 million acres poisoned by
salt residue resulting from poor drainage, and to
address the problems of 400,000 acres in the San
Joaquin Valley. A fourth of this land was already in
critical stages, showing a 20 to 30 percent decline in
productivity.

But all of Dr. Grew's goals had to be abandoned
at least temporarily because the soil conservation

program was *rejected* by the state legislators. "Yes, it was a big disappointment," Dr. Grew admitted, when I pressed her, "but I'd like to believe that at least we have created the awareness that there is a very serious problem. That may not sound like much to you, but until very recently my colleagues actually thought there was no problem, even though we are already showing the classic early signs of desertification. We just have to keep trying to find a plan that they will understand and approve. When you are working on frontier issues, you are often ahead of your constituency."

Dr. Grew hopes that it will be possible to get people to respond before there is a disaster. "We need to take heed of the fall of North Africa which was once the granary of Rome," she told me, and then she explained that California had a climate that is almost identical with the climate of the Mediterranean. "Without a halt to these problems," she added, "California's farmlands could go out of production like Mesopotamia or North Africa, which both became barren wastelands."

With some variation in degree, the same conditions prevail from coast to coast. All across America the land is in danger of losing its ability to produce food. In Iowa, for example, a state that produces one-tenth of the nation's food and more than 20 percent of our food exports, farmers are losing two bushels of soil for every bushel of corn. Erosion losses average three times what is acceptable. Iowa has already lost half of its resource base. In the Southeast, the Pacific Northwest, New England, and almost everywhere that food is grown, American agriculture is at risk. Erosion, combined with the destruction of land for the building of dams, for urbanization and other

179

uses, creates a pattern which will inevitably result in dangerous and massive food shortages if it is allowed to continue.

Every time American agriculture loses one and one-third acres of cropland, another baby is born. The connection isn't direct, but it dramatizes a problem: Population is growing, farmland is shrinking, and per-acre crop yields on the land that is left are leveling off.[27]

For the first time in our national history experts are publicly predicting this nation's agricultural decline.

"I think it is highly unlikely that our great-grandchildren will believe that there was ever a surplus of food in the United States," predicted John Turner, soil conservation officer for Monroe County, Missouri. And speaking in Washington, then Secretary of Agriculture Bob Bergland added, "If something is not done about the land it will be barren."

9 Poisoning the Food

Fathers and mothers and children, farmers and factory workers, the aged and the vigorous are affected and, with some exceptions, the slow drop-by-drop, breath-by-breath contamination progresses unseen and unheard.
—Ronald B. Taylor, *The Poisoning of America*

The men who worked close to the soil should have seen the changes in the land coming, and some of them did. But more often than not the extensive use of chemicals had kept farm yields so high that for many years they masked both the damage of erosion and the importance of preserving prime farmland. There had always been enough rich, fertile,

181

highly productive soil to keep farmers from worrying about how long the chemicals could compensate for man's abuse—or how dangerous using them might turn out to be.

A few people did express deep concern, not about a drop in productivity nor about the destruction of the land but about the human price of chemical agriculture, the slow, cumulative poisoning of America, through its food supply.

In the early sixties, marine biologist and science writer Rachel Carson warned in *Silent Spring* about the dangers of expanding the use of chemicals, which she called "a bright new toy whose harmful effects might not be felt for twenty or more years." Now the "harmful effects" that she feared are becoming obvious.

Most of our foods are coated with pesticides that were developed to kill *living creatures*. Despite the warnings of experts, we collectively accepted the assurance of the chemical industries that those chemicals would not injure or kill *us*. But today a trend is clearly emerging. Thousands of people are developing bizarre and previously unknown illnesses which they firmly believe are caused by our agricultural chemicals.

Now, at a time when America's agriculture is already being severely threatened by energy availability and by land losses, serious new evidence indicates that many agricultural chemicals that have increased the food supply may have to be abandoned. Basic methods of producing food may have to change. That change would inevitably cause food shortages and it would create additional hunger.

Nevertheless, no matter how much we don't want to change, the American people may soon *have* to choose between living without those chemicals and

182

thus living with less food, or accepting the risks of miscarriages, deformed children, stillbirths, festering sores, cancer, and strange changes in personality. These conditions have already been linked to some of our agricultural chemicals with a frequency and a regularity that can no longer be ignored.

In some cases we can still say that the final proof isn't in. We can insist on waiting until we have that proof, but enough concern has already been generated to have caused Douglas M. Costle, then head of the Environmental Protection Agency, to sign an emergency order on February 28, 1979, suspending the use of the agricultural chemical 2,4,5-T after it had been connected to a series of miscarriages among women living in Oregon's Alsea Basin area. That was after eight women wrote to the Environmental Protection Agency complaining that they had suffered ten spontaneous abortions since 1973 and that each of the abortions occurred in the spring after the spraying of the herbicides 2,4,5-T and 2,4-D in nearby forests. The Environmental Protection Agency investigated the charges and found that there was a strong correlation between the spraying and the reported abortions. Then the agency conducted a second study of a wider area within the forests of Lincoln, Lane, and Benton counties, and it concluded that the "Abortion rate index is significantly higher" than in areas where the herbicides had not been used.

These findings came after more than thirty years of widespread use and more than ten years of complaints by the area's residents and physicians. And even then, only 2,4,5-T was taken off the market; 2,4-D is still being tested by the Environmental Protection Agency. And in the meantime it is still being marketed, sold, and inhaled, even though many area residents and physicians believe that it, too, must also be taken off the market.

Dr. Barbara Wood, the Lincoln County health officer, conducted a survey and concluded that there had been a "definite increase in all the symptoms" after a spraying of the areas crops with 2,4-D. The National Cancer Institute's Frederick Cancer Research Center in Maryland reviewed all laboratory tests on 2,4-D and concluded that 2,4-D is a carcinogen and causes reproductive problems. A large number of Oregon residents have had direct experience that supports those findings.

Many families who lived in an Oregon forest area sprayed with 2,4-D have had deformed children. Drs. Renee and Chuck Stringham, alone, have delivered nineteen malformed infants. One of those babies looked normal at birth, but they soon found that it had a defect in its skull. There was a small hole between his brain cavity and the frontal sinus that allowed a portion of the brain to protrude. It also caused repeated bouts of spinal meningitis which resulted in blindness and deafness. The condition has been treated, but no one knows to what extent the child's brain has been damaged. The physicians are convinced that there is sufficient evidence to connect the agricultural sprayings of 2,4-D with this birth defect and with the other birth defects that they are seeing.[28]

Dr. Charles F. Wurster of the National Cancer Institute in Washington, D.C., has asked the chemical companies to withdraw the chemicals that are thought to be unsafe, at least until they can be tested. "Chemicals are not innocent until proven guilty," he said, "and if you consider a chemical innocent until proven guilty, then the people are going to have to get tumors to prove it guilty."[29]

Actually that is exactly what is happening. The chemical companies are not withdrawing their chemicals, and although they are receiving very little public attention, many American farmers are getting tumors and other illnesses that are associated with the chemicals that they spray. If you spend time in the American farm belt, before long you are likely to hear stories of poisonings, miscarriages, strange behavior, illnesses, tumors, and deaths that the farmers and their families believe are linked to pesticides.

Stories like this one: The wind was blowing hard the day that grain and cattle farmer Harry Rowell sprayed his wheat crop with methyl parathion. Shortly after he had finished he felt his face and lips become numb. Other symptoms rapidly followed. Rowell became extremely weak and tired; soon he could barely walk. Harry Rowell never recovered. Doctors found the cause of his death perplexing, so on his death certificate they recorded liver failure as the primary cause and listed the chemical methyl parathion as a "toxic secondary" cause.

Since there is no reliable system of collecting or reporting information on chemical poisoning in the United States, it is hard to prove the actual cause of such deaths. But from time to time a farmer who has become ill after using a specific chemical has decided to take the manufacturer to court.

Alphy Menold is one such farmer. In the fall of 1977 the Princeville, Illinois, grain farmer filed a three-million-dollar suit against the American Cyanamid Company, alleging that the firm's insecticide, Counter 15 G, caused "acute toxic poisoning resulting in hypoplastic anemia and acute tubular necrosis." The lawsuit contends that the chemical is unsafe for its recommended use and that the package doesn't give adequate warning of its hazards. Menold was hospitalized in April 1977 after two days of planting corn with the insecticide and reportedly following all of the instructions on the label. On the second day, while he was working, he became violently ill. He began to vomit, his vision blurred, and he had intense pain in his chest and stomach. Alphy Menold died shortly after taking the chemical company to court.[30] Today his wife is continuing the lawsuit.

In some cases, feed animals have been the victims of the chemicals. George Neary, a farmer and rancher with a 45,000-acre ranch near Sacramento Valley in Northern California, blames the death of hundreds of his cows on toxaphene, a chemical that was sprayed on his animals by the U.S. States Department of Agriculture *without* his consent. In late 1978, as Neary tells it, the USDA and various state counterparts decided that American cattle were experiencing an epidemic of scabies or mange, an illness that makes the cattle itch. The USDA formally announced an eradication program which involved dipping all of the cattle in the United States in toxaphene at a cost to the American taxpayers of roughly $126 million a year. The program was supposed to continue for as long as it took to eradicate scabies.

"My ranch was the first in Northern California that they approached," Neary explained in an interview.

They were aware that none of my cattle had scabies and that I was away in Oregon on business. When they arrived they told my wife that it didn't matter that none of my cows were sick, because this was part of their training program and that they could use federal marshals and force if she resisted.

That was a Tuesday. When I returned three days later, my cattle were showing all of the classic signs of poisoning. Animals were falling down, they were walking backwards, and staggering. Over the next few months one hundred and thirty of our mature cows died.

Neary was right. The damage had been caused by toxaphene, an irrevocable neurotoxin which the Department of Agriculture had purchased from Hercules, Inc., in Wilmington, Delaware. The deaths didn't stop with the mature cows, they went on and on.

We had between seven hundred and eight hundred abortions or stillbirths. Our ranch became like a giant morgue. Even the mature cows that survived were sick and suffering. They dropped in weight from roughly one thousand one hundred pounds down to seven hundred pounds. Their digestive processes had been destroyed.

To be blunt, I think that the FDA, USDA, EPA, and the big chemical companies are all swapping favors in a kind of chemical musical chairs game. They owe each other these favors because a lot of the upper echelon of EPA was drawn out of USDA. Much of USDA, in turn, came directly from industry. They scratch each other's backs. The chemical companies put up millions to support USDA activities and in turn USDA buys and uses their poisons.

Yes, ma'am, I believe that is the real reason that USDA intended to spray *every* cow in America, a hundred and fifty million cows, when only four hundred seventy-seven cows had the condition. In California, alone, they were planning to spray five to ten million cows when they only had evidence that two cows had the disease. You have to admit it's the perfect bureaucratic technique. First, they find a nonproblem, then they spend an enormous amount of money on it, the money goes to their friends at the chemical company, and then when they have paid back their favors and want some Brownie points from the American public, they announce that they have solved the problem.

I am suing the Department of Agriculture. They are countersuing. But at least I have the satisfaction of knowing that I have stopped this particular reckless program. They were actually spraying chemical wastes on the cows that we slaughter and the American people eat—at a cost of a hundred million dollars. I'm very bitter about it because I understand that, in effect, the taxpayer was paying for his own poison. If those wastes had not been sprayed on our cattle or consumed on our vegetables, it would have been necessary to store them in places like Love Canal.

The USDA thinks that it controls the cornucopia, but I think that it is out of control. Its methods are dangerous. It is true we are producing animals for slaughter in half the time that we once did. But the fetal abnormalities in those animals have gone up nine hundred percent in the last ten years. Naturally, no one has done a study on this frolic in chemical agriculture, and no one knows to what extent we are poisoning our own products and being poisoned ourselves.

The controversy over the USDA's poisoning of George Neary's cattle became offically known as "high-level episode 6TEH-79." Actually, toxaphene has been used for thirty years in smaller doses than the one which killed Neary's cattle. American farmers have sprayed an estimated forty to one hundred million pounds of it to control insects on cotton, on vegetables, and on livestock. Yet, until recently, almost nothing was known about its effects. On March 16, 1979, after studying toxaphene for six years, the National Cancer Institute reported that toxaphene caused cancer in both male and female mice. Test results also suggested that the toxaphene caused thyroid cancer in rats.

Other scientists who specialize in toxiology have taken a stronger stand than the National Cancer Institute. Dr. Adrian Gross, DVM, formerly associate director of the Food and Drug Administration's scientific investigations unit, said that the test data made it "abundantly clear" that toxaphene is an extremely potent carcinogen in rats as well as in mice, and added that he had never before encountered an agent "purposefully introduced into the environment . . . which had a carcinogenic propensity as clearly marked and as pervasive." Dr. Melvin Reuber, MD, an Environmental Protection Agency consultant, said, "Toxaphene is such a carcinogen it boggles the mind. Anything that is shown to be dangerous in animals, has to be dangerous in humans."[31] John P. Frawely, the corporate director of toxicology at Hercules Chemicals, the company that sold the toxaphene, disagreed. He contended that the studies on mice should all be discounted since mice develop tumors very easily without agents like toxaphene.

The problem is not a simple one. The use of toxaphene alone causes the nation's farmers to increase food production by about $1 billion a year. If toxaphene is taken off the market, each year a billion dollars' worth of food will also be lost from the American food supply.

Meanwhile, the Environmental Protection Agency has begun to record toxaphene poisonings of farm workers, farmers, and pesticide sprayers. It has recently attributed eight agricultural deaths directly to contact with toxaphene. The EPA has also conducted commodity survey tests which have revealed a "slow but steady rise" in the amount of toxaphene that the American public consumes. Residues now are found in leaf and stem vegetables and especially in fish sold in supermarkets across America. The EPA has concluded "it is apparent . . . that toxaphene contaminates both vegetables and fish and remains in the soils for as long as 14 years, making hazardous accumulation in soil and air a possibility."

In Arizona, milk supplies were contaminated

with toxaphene. In 1979 Governor Bruce Babbitt discovered that the Arizona Health Department had been aware of the contamination for a long time and had suppressed the news. "I found my Health Department was not releasing the information. They were keeping the information to themselves . . . the Dairy Commissioner was in up to his ears. He had known for years that the stuff was contaminated. It was an enormous problem."[32]

Most of the safety advice that farmers receive about spraying their crops and livestock with toxaphene and with other chemicals is limited to the container labels. Usually the labels recommend that the farmers wear protective clothing and they contain cautions against poisoning, but they don't warn the farmer about the long-term effects on the people who handle the chemicals or on the people who eat the products. That kind of information is available only in technical journals on toxicology. For that reason, Nebraska's *New Land Review* conducted its own study, intended especially for farmers, and published a list of the long-term risks of common insecticides and herbicides. The study found that almost every one of the most commonly used insecticides and herbicides had been linked with mutations, birth defects or other serious conditions.

The illnesses and the deaths associated with these agricultural chemicals are likely to increase since each year more and more chemicals have to be sprayed on the food in order to control the rapidly rising number of insects that have become resistant to the chemicals.

During the past thirty years, pesticide use in this country has increased more than tenfold. Yet, despite that, massive increases in insect-caused losses to standing crops have almost doubled.[33] The chemicals are failing to work as they once did. Chemically resistant strains of insects are multiplying and increases in productivity are beginning to fall off.

George Ware, a research scientist at the University of Arizona, has been suggesting a ban on toxaphene simply because over the years most of the bugs have become immune to it and are no longer affected. As a result, farmers have to use heavier concentrations or mix two or more chemical compounds together in an effort to create more deadly combinations.

Ignorance about the effects of these chemicals on people should be sufficient reason for caution. The indication that human life may be in danger and that the chemicals might have devastating and unforeseen effects suggests that it would be logical to stop using them until we are sure. But agricultural experts say that we can't stop. "Deny agronomists the use of chemical aids and the world will be doomed . . . ," warned Nobel Prize-winning scientist, Dr. Norman Borlaug. Even J. I. Rodale, of the Rodale Press, whose organic research enterprises earned him millions of dollars and the title of the Prophet of American Organic Agriculture, believed that the arguments that organic farming can be done on a large scale were highly exaggerated and based on a very selective choice of facts. He said that organic methods of composting and cultivation were not suitable for large corporate farms and probably couldn't be done on a large scale.[34]

In the words of Rachel Carson, "Can anyone believe it is possible to lay down such a barrage of poisons on the surface of the earth without making it unfit for all life?"[35]

192

III
The Solutions

Man possesses, for a small moment in his history, the most powerful combination of knowledge, tools, and resources the world has ever known. He has all that is physically necessary to create a totally new form of human society—one that would be built to last for generations.

—Club of Rome, *The Limits to Growth*

10 Taking Charge

I learned from my two years' experiment that it would cost incredibly little trouble to obtain one's necessary food even in this latitude, that many a man may use as simple a diet as the animals and yet retain health and strength.
—Henry David Thoreau, *Walden*, 1854

Americans have had too many years of taking the risks that the chemical companies calculate, and too many years of accepting the rising cost of food and the increasing scarcity of food that land destruction and energy hoarding have caused.

The United States government is permitting, in fact is encouraging, this nation to drift from one

ecological, political, and economic crisis to another.
Now we are entering a period of increased agricultural vulnerability in both the long term and the
short term.

Many of the chemicals we depend on for high
food yields will have to be abandoned as their dangers continue to be discovered. This problem is com-
pounded by the decreasing harvests for major crops
which indicate that we can no longer expect better
yields from soils that are being abused.

It is also clear that if it continues, the loss of
essential farmland through erosion will result in desertification and severely reduced productivity. It
should be apparent to policymakers that we will need
every bit of good land that we have left, and yet this
nation continues to turn on itself and destroy its own
best, currently planted prime farmland, even as
supplies and reserves are diminishing and population
and food demands are increasing.

To make matters worse, our social and economic
systems continue to permit the oil and natural gas
that are used in every phase of the agricultural cycle
to be controlled by an energy anarchy that leaves our
food production and distribution at the mercy of the
OPEC nations and the large U.S. oil companies.

As these developments and threats converge,
the food supply of the American people, not just the
American poor, becomes increasingly unstable. Before we are badly damaged by chemicals, before the
rest of our rich farmland is destroyed through carelessness, poor planning, abuse, and greed, before our
oil supplies are further manipulated and the risk of
massive, uncontrollable hunger becomes a reality,
the American people need to find and implement
answers.

It is especially important that we, the people, do

something, because our government has made absolutely no plans for possible food shortages or for any
kind of agricultural crisis. In fact, Harold Gay, chief
food planner for the Department of Agriculture in the
Carter administration, acknowledged in October 1980
that we have no nationally owned food stockpiles—
and no emergency food reserve. "There are individ-
ually owned farmer reserves," he said, "but the average American city has just what is in its supermarkets and in its wholesalers' warehouses. That is
about a nine-day retail supply and ten-day wholesale
supply of staple items. Those numbers are based on
normal buying patterns. In a crisis the supply would
be gone much faster."

I knew that was true. I had seen it happen. On
the day of the accident at the nuclear reactor on
Three Mile Island, near Middletown, Pennsylvania,
my local supermarket, eighty miles away from the
scene of the crisis, was emptied in a matter of hours.
People jammed the store and bought everything in
sight.

Sometimes people ask me what there is to be
done. I tell them I think that there are three crucial
issues. The first is to be protected against the danger
of sudden and extreme shortages or price increases.
The second is to find a way to get good food and
enough of it to the people who are hungry in this
country right now. The third is to choose and to
implement long-term solutions to the agricultural
and ecological crises that threaten us.

The first is the easiest. It just means keeping an
extra supply of food around that can provide people
with the kind of security and peace of mind that they
need before they move on to do more. By that I mean
the knowledge that whatever happens to the supply,

the cost, or availability of food, they can, at least for a while, have something for themselves and their children to eat.

Ideally, every family should have enough food stored or accessible to survive for one agricultural cycle, roughly a year. The Mormons have traditionally done this. But if that is not possible even a small amount is better than none. The Russians, I am told, have enough food stored to feed their entire population for a year. Much of that food came from America.

There are several ways to go about storing food. The simplest and most efficient method for people who do not have much free time or storage space is simply to buy a supply of freeze-dried foods. Freeze-dried food contains no added chemicals or preservatives. It does not need to be cooked and it lasts for many years. It can be stored in about one-fourth to one-seventh the amount of space that an equivalent amount of fresh food would take. A year's supply for a family of four can be stored in an average-sized coat closet.

People who live in the suburbs or in the country and have even a small amount of land can buy certain basics like wheat, powdered milk, honey, and salt, and grow much of the rest of what they need to be self-sufficient.

A couple of fruit trees and a garden of about ten feet by fifteen feet can provide enough fresh food to feed an average family. The seeds cost only a few dollars. Recent figures from the National Garden Bureau point out that the vegetables you can grow in a fifteen-by-twenty-five-foot garden would cost $284 at 1980 supermarket prices. The seeds for that garden would cost only $9.80. Today, one small, well-kept garden can assure a harvest of food. People can

easily save the seeds from this yield to plant again
and harvest again.

Food that is grown in the spring and summer
can be stored for winter. Many fruits like apples,
apricots, prunes, and figs can be sun-dried on hot
days. Most fruits and vegetables can also be stored in
any cool dry place between 30 and 50 degrees F. Part
of a basement or toolshed, even an old trunk or
plastic bucket partially buried and covered with
straw or dirt, can be used.

Even people who live in apartments can grow
food as long as a rooftop, a windowsill, a patio, or
just a doorstep is available. They can raise vegetables in containers and harvest them year round.
Actually, almost anything that can be grown in a
garden can also be grown in a container. For people
in the cities there is also community gardening. By
that I mean three or more people gardening on land
they don't own. Right now there are about two
million community gardeners in the United States.
Some communities share the expense and establish
canning centers that the entire community can use.

At the Blue Grass CAA Cannery Nutrition
Center in Lawrenceburg, Kentucky, more than 10,000
jars of food are processed each summer by local
residents. Many of the community's elderly people
also have gardens planted with free seeds donated by
the Elderly Gardening Opportunity Program. On any
typical day women and children and the elderly can
be seen carrying bags, boxes and buckets of vegetables into the center to put up food for the winter
ahead.

What I am really trying to get at is the
importance of not remaining passive and at the
mercy of a food supply we can't control and yet can't
survive without. Many American people have lost

sight of the land and what is happening to it. They have lost sight of the way that food is grown and harvested and packaged and carried to the stores where they finally buy it, and I think they have also lost sight of the fact that someday it might not be there. Most Americans have not thought very much about these things and that leaves them unprepared and less able—in fact, far less—able to cope with sudden shortages than those who have long survived on very little and slowly learned to endure the deprivation.

Learning how and preparing to get through an acute crisis is only the first part of what must be done. The second is realizing that wherever you live, chronically hungry families live nearby. It is possible to find and help these people. It is clearly more difficult than simply storing food for oneself, and some people think it is work that is only suited to a few religious leaders or charities, but that is not the case. All of us can work toward ending hunger.

The Hunger Project is a nonprofit agency, composed of people dedicated to ending hunger in America and the world. Anyone can join. The concept is simple. The Hunger Project informs and educates the public about the facts of the world hunger problem. The organization asks its members to take whatever action they can toward ending hunger. It believes that the mobilization of the popular will to end hunger can transform the world's ability to handle the problem. It maintains that a collection of individual activities directed toward this common goal has the power to make a great difference.

Since its inception in 1977 more than one million seven hundred thousand people have enrolled in the Hunger Project and have stated their commitment to ending hunger. That membership, now the largest hunger-related group in the world, has become a powerful vehicle able to create far-reaching political and social change.

There really is no reason why anyone who wants to cannot help to solve the problems of the hungry. Over the years I have met many people who made up their minds to be responsive to the broken hopes and unmet needs of others. The attitudes and efforts of these people have created changes of enormous proportions.

One middle-aged, middle-class mother whom I met recently in Northeast Philadelphia is, with help from her friends, feeding 308 of the most isolated, poor, and previously hungry people in her area. She is doing it with no federal funding and no government help. Rita Schiavone's explanation is better than mine because it comes from her direct experience.

"I got involved in hunger when my youngest child started first grade," she told me. "One day I was sitting at home doing housework and I thought to myself, What am I really doing for anyone? I mean, what am I doing that is really meaningful? I had heard that the Cardinal's Commission on Human Relations needed help, and after thinking about it for a while I decided to volunteer. I began to make calls on the poor, the handicapped, the isolated, and the old. Before long I found a woman with no food. I was shocked by that, and I ran out and bought her a sandwich. That night as I cooked dinner for my family I thought about her and how much better it would be to take her some of the food I was cooking. I put some aside and I brought it to her the next day. I didn't know it at the time, but that was the first meal of what we would later call Aid for Friends."

Rita Schiavone began to look further and

learned that there were many other hungry people in her community. She spoke to friends and neighbors and asked them to cook a little extra food whenever they could. Ed Piszek, owner of Mrs. Paul's frozen foods, heard about her work and offered to supply trays for freezing the food. The following year an article in the *Philadelphia Evening Bulletin* brought contact with others. The idea took hold and started growing.

Today hundreds of thousands of meals have been served. The women don't ask people who have requested food any questions or make them fill out any forms. They realize that some people who don't really need the food might be getting it, but they believe that it is better to take people at their word and to feed someone who doesn't need their help than to deprive or embarrass someone who does.

Since the program's inception, almost four thousand people have contributed food. Volunteers are asked to cook one or more extra servings each week while preparing meals for their families. One woman puts the tray on the dinner table and says to her children, "This food is for our unseen guest." Volunteers collect the frozen dinners each week and take them to central freezers, then other volunteers pick up a week's supply of dinners and deliver them. The volunteer also stays and visits for at least an hour each week. That way the people feel less alone.

"Just as a mother takes care of her children and nurtures. them, I believe that we have to have an extended family and nurture others," Rita Schiavone said. "It is inherent in our humanity; that's what sets us apart from the animals. I gave up my dream to go back to college and get a degree in music, but I have gained a great deal. I think I have gained more than a degree could ever have given me."

Rita Schiavone has also given a great deal, given more than food; actually she has given some part of herself. So has Morton Waber.

One night in May 1968, Waber, a short, gray-haired conservatively dressed man, a part owner of a Philadelphia insurance firm, sat down after dinner to watch television. His regular program was preempted that night by a CBS special report, *Hunger in America*. It depicted Southern blacks who were hungry, migrant workers up North who were hungry—and hungry kids who were apathetic, brain-damaged, and unable to learn. That film was to change Morton Waber's life.

"My God!" he said to his wife. "There are actually children in this country who are going hungry!"

"So?" his wife asked. "So what are you going to do about it?"

"Well, I don't know," Waber answered honestly, "but I'm not going to turn off the television and forget it."

The next day his wife, a slender, middle-aged woman, went to teach her poverty-level kindergarten children with the documentary still in her mind. Troubled, one of the first things she asked that morning was, "How many of you don't eat breakfast?"

A number of children raised their hands. Suddenly, Mrs. Waber thought she knew at least one reason why some of the kids were always restless and why they weren't learning. When she came home that night, she told her husband, "I think my kids can't keep their minds on their work because they're hungry." Her husband's face lit up.

"I'll feed them," he said.

The next morning Waber was there at the Drew School at Thirty-eighth Street and Powelton Avenue, talking to the principal. "I understand you have some hungry kids. I want to feed them," he said.

He'd figured on feeding maybe fifteen or twenty kids, but the principal just smiled. "Three-quarters of the children in this school are hungry every day."

"If that's the case then I'll feed them all," Waber said. "I don't know how I'll do it, but I will; somehow I'll feed them all."

Sealtest got the first phone call. "How much will it cost me to give four hundred and fifty kids milk and orange juice every morning?" Waber asked.

"You want to do this out of your own pocket?" inquired the incredulous voice at the other end of the phone.

Bond Bread was next, and Waber got the same surprised reaction. It is likely that the executives in these companies were touched by Waber's intentions, because the food was given at cost and delivered each morning to Waber, who waited alone in the school-yard of the Drew School and carried the food to each classroom personally.

That's how Morton Waber began, single-handedly, to feed some of the children of Philadelphia. The first four weeks of the program cost him a thousand dollars and, in return, one little girl wrote him a letter which asked, "What makes a man like you care about a kid like me?"

During the summer, Waber turned the program into a tax-deductible charity called "Food for Thought." He got friends to contribute. The next year he heard that the Department of Agriculture had a plan that would pay 80 percent of the cost of a food program if half of a school's students were living below the poverty level. Waber applied for the allocation and he got it. This allowed him to feed five times as many children. When the program continued to expand, the Junior Chamber of Commerce started to provide people to help Waber distribute the cereal, the orange juice, the milk, and the vitamin-fortified cakes. That was the beginning of the free breakfast program.

Today every school in Philadelphia with poverty-level kids is eligible.

Of course, it's not just kids who are vulnerable and need help. Hundreds of senior citizens in Sacramento, California, decided to face up to their own economic and nutritional vulnerability. They set up a nonprofit organization which received no funding of any kind, was totally self-supporting and still managed to provide food for its twelve hundred members and have enough left over to serve forty-five local charities. They did it quite simply—by collecting the food that the rest of society was throwing away.

These "Gleaners" go into the fields of nearby farms after the machines and migrant workers have gone and they harvest the food that has been left behind to rot. Farmers who learn that they can get Internal Revenue Service credit for giving food to a charity are usually pleased to have the Gleaners come, and often they purposely save food that they can't sell so that the Gleaners can collect it. There are, for example, strict rules governing the sale of fruit. Ordinarily in Sacramento, undersized fruit would just be thrown away. Supermarkets, too, have joined the farmers and often give the Gleaners fruits and vegetables that are not salable but are still good enough to eat. The Gleaners, who operate rent free out of a condemned school, also get tons and tons of frozen or canned food that has passed the expiration date but has not yet spoiled.

Sometimes a bakery will overbake and the Gleaners will get a call and rush over with huge plastic bags to pick up doughnuts or bread or cake.

Since they never know what is coming in, someone
has to be available twenty-four hours a day. In
addition to volunteering time, each member pays two
dollars a month. That's how the gas and telephone
and overhead are paid for. "Everyone benefits from
this pro-gram," explained Gleaner Arlene Paule.
"The farmers and storekeepers feel better and get tax
deductions. The old people feel useful. We let people
do what they are comfortable doing. I myself am
partially disabled. I'm not able to climb ladders, but
nuts and cherries and apples fall to the ground. I can
root around on the ground and pack bags and bags of
food that would otherwise have rotted there. The food
helps an awful lot of people to survive in these hard
times. I think there is a tremendous power in what
we do. In our case it was a spontaneous activity that
had arisen out of need. Our moral commitment is to
avoid waste. It could be done anywhere in America.
Actually, it *is* being done in many parts of America.
Food banks based on similar concepts now stretch
from coast to coast. They are linked by a National
Salvage Food Bank Network, called Second Harvest.
Meetings are held around the country so that food-
bank operators can exchange ideas and help to get
new food banks started. The philosophy of the group
is simply this: The poor shall always be with us but
why the hungry?"

Not every effort to help the hungry works out so
well. The Little Brothers of the Poor, a storefront
operation on Belmont Avenue in Chicago, is one of a
number of independent, grass-roots organizations
staffed by people who donate their time and try to
help and feed the city's hungry and poor.

Sometimes by the time they learn about such
people it's too late. The codirector explained that she
had received a call the day before from a woman who

sold groceries in the National food store. The woman asked her to try to find a man named John Ness. She said she was worried because he always came to the store looking for food that they discarded but she had not seen him for several days. She knew the block he lived on but not the house. "I went looking," the codirector said. "I walked up and down the street asking people where he lived. At first nobody seemed to know the old man. Finally, someone directed me to a basement slum; all the windows were plastic, filthy, dirty, and half torn down. I had food in my hands. I stood at the broken-down door and I thought, Oh, my God, nobody can live in this place. I guess I was right. It turned out he had died there two days before."

No one knows how many John Nesses there are in each city in America. Often they die in their rooms after malnutrition has weakened their bodies. There are no statistics showing how many times these people have sought help. But it is clear that the need is great and that the city of Chicago has done more toward meeting it than many other cities.

In Chicago there are, for example, over a hundred privately funded food pantries which keep in touch through a single emergency-food-distribution network and provide a free supply of food to anyone who is in danger of starving.

The Lakeview Food Pantry is one of them. Located in the Jane Addams Center at 3212 N. Broadway, the small brightly painted room is staffed completely by volunteers. Food and money are donated by churches, community organizations, schools, and stores that sometimes contribute their unsalable items, like dented cans or old bread. A few people send monthly checks.

Inside, a young man sat with his child, a boy of about seven. Next to him, a woman without stockings stood wrapped in a heavy winter coat. An old unshaven man chatted with a former psychologist who had had a mental breakdown four years before and still could not find work.

They all watched quietly as a slender Mexican girl with waist-length black hair entered the pantry. "I need some food for my baby, please." She said 'please' as if she were expecting to have to beg.

"Do you have any food for yourself?" the volunteer asked gently?

"No," the girl answered, "but I hate to take it for myself; to me the baby is more important."

Then she explained that she was only sixteen and the baby's father had disappeared. She had applied for government aid but had been told that she must wait until she was eighteen before she could get it. "I can't wait two years. My baby is starving now," she said. "I don't want her to die." She was given a bag of food. They all were. One at a time each of these people held out their empty paper bags and had them filled with a two-day supply of food.

It is clear that if hunger in America is to end we must have more involved individuals, more food pantries, more Little Brothers of the Poor, more Gleaners, and more individuals like Rita Schiavone and Morton Waber. It is also clear that the government of the future will do less, much less, than the government of the past. In addition to cutting the budget in areas where hunger and suffering were already extensive, the Reagan administration has remained blind to the present reality of hunger and poverty in America. In December 1980 Martin Anderson, Ronald Reagan's chief adviser on domestic affairs, announced that poverty had been "virtually wiped out in the United States, our systems of government aid had been a brilliant success," he said and then he added that *they should now be dismantled.*"[36]

11 Ending Hunger

I have the audacity to believe that peoples everywhere can have three meals a day. . . . I believe that what self-centered men have torn down other-centered men can build up. I still believe that one day mankind will bow before the altars of God and be crowned triumphant. . . . I still believe that we shall overcome.
—Martin Luther King, Jr.
Nobel Peace Prize Acceptance Speech

Nothing will be more difficult than implementing the changes that could solve the long-term problems of hunger, changes that could preserve the land, and use existing techniques, that would make it possible for this country to feed itself and help the world.

209

It is not that all of these changes are inherently difficult; many are surprisingly simple, but they involve giving up some old and deeply rooted ways. Powerful groups which still benefit and grow rich from current practices will not want to see them changed. Many of those who do not benefit will also resist the changes, simply because people are slow when it comes to giving up what they know and turning things around.

Yet it is clear to most of us, when we stop and think about it, that America has a responsibility that is far-reaching and vital. If major harvests or distribution systems in this country fail, millions in other countries will starve and die. Even if major harvests or distribution systems do not fail, America must find new ways to produce much more food on much less land with much less energy, or as the population increases, millions will starve, here and abroad.

There are times in history when choices are made that change the future of a country forever. This is one of those times. So far, America has pursued short-term gain at great human and ecological cost. The country can continue on this path for a while longer—and follow it to disaster.

The American people can watch history repeat itself. We can become one of many civilizations that prospered for a few centuries and then were destroyed: countries like ours with rich farmland, with lakes and with abundant food supplies, civilizations whose remnants can now be found only in our museums. Rome and North Africa followed this route, but Americans are destroying the essential core of their food-producing system faster than any people who have ever lived.

Much of the destruction of land and topsoil that has already taken place is irreversible. Some people hope that hydroponics—growing food in tanks of nutrient-enriched water instead of soil—giant food factories, research in genetic engineering and future advances in plant chemistry will save us. But the truth is that we do not have to wait; answers exist right now, only so far most of them have been ignored or suppressed.

Dr. John Ryther, a highly respected and well-known marine biologist at the Woods Hole (Massachusetts) Oceanographic Institution, points out that there are about one billion acres of coastal wetlands in the world. If only one-tenth of these wetlands were used to raise fish, the potential yield of fish using improved methods of production would be one hundred million tons a year. This is the equivalent of the yield from the entire world's commercial fisheries.

Dr. Ryther has also devised a complex continuous culture system which produces oysters, seaweed, worms, flounder, and abalone. It ultimately becomes a biological sewage treatment plant returning clean water to the sea.

If this kind of system were implemented on a large scale it could produce a million pounds of shellfish a year from each one-acre production facility. By using advanced culture techniques like those developed at Woods Hole, Dr. Ryther estimates that the yield could well be multiplied tenfold within the next three decades.

So far no one in America has done anything about implementing these concepts. Dr. Ryther, who has quietly been working on ways to improve fish production in the ocean for fifteen years, explained patiently, "I don't expect anything different. Innovations often take a long time. I think that aquaculture will be very important in the food supply of the future. Already I can see that things are beginning to change. There is a little bit less waste than there used to be. Fish like mullet are beginning to be accepted by Americans. Right now, outside my window," he added, "a fleet of boats are fishing for squid, which will be sent overseas. Most of the catch could provide excellent food for us. It just takes time for Americans to come around to realizing that."

Actually, what has been done to the supply of fish closely mirrors what has been done in agriculture. There was a short period of very high productivity followed by depletion, and then decline and long-term damage. Between 1850 and 1950 the fish catch increased tenfold. It doubled again between 1950 and 1960 and again between 1960 and 1970. But in 1970 development began to slow down, and then slowly after that, decline of the favored species set in.

Scientists from the United Nations Food and Agriculture Organization had warned that such huge catches could not be sustained, but instead of responding to the warnings, bigger and bigger ships with more sophisticated and costlier fishing gear continued to deplete a supply that once seemed boundless. Even after the yields of fish began to fall, the industry responded with more and more gadgetry. Today hydrophones make high-fidelity recordings of fish sounds which are then analyzed by communications specialists who isolate the bait-catching noises. After that the recordings are played by powerful sound projectors in order to attract fish over wide distances and lure them to their deaths. Remote telemetering systems listen to fish calls and report the areas with the largest concentrations of fish.

Then, completely computerized and automated fishing fleets go into action after being triggered by computers programmed to respond to the telemetric buoys.

But it doesn't work. With all this technology and expensive equipment, the fisheries catch less than they could have caught with fewer ships in fewer hours and at less expense. In the salmon fisheries of the United States and Canada the same yearly catch could be achieved for about $50 million less each year than is currently being spent. The shrimp industry offers another example of the same kind of self-defeating activity. In 1950, one hundred boats fishing off the Gulf of California each caught about one hundred tons of shrimp a year. By 1975, there were eight hundred shrimp boats fishing in that area and each one caught less than twenty tons of shrimp a year.

While depleting the ocean of certain species of fish we are needlessly wasting other edible species. Donald R. Whitier, of the National Marine Fisheries Service, has pointed out that for every pound of shrimp we catch, five to ten pounds of edible fish are actually hauled in, and then instead of being marketed they are dumped back into the sea as unsalable. If we simply kept these fish, which are mostly squid, skate, croaker, and hake, they alone could provide much of the food needed to feed hungry Americans. The wasted fish in United States waters contain enough fish protein concentrate to provide supplemental animal protein to one billion people for three hundred days at a cost of less than one-half cent a day per person.[37]

The food supply from the sea could be increased fifty- to a hundredfold. All that is really needed is a decision on the part of the policymakers and the industrialists of this country to stop wasting it. That is also the case with the land. Only more so. In America we presently grow and then virtually throw away the food that could feed the world.

Soybeans are the richest source of natural protein of all foods, including meat. Soybeans can sustain and nourish human life. They offer unlimited potential, but for the most part they are not being sold, marketed, or eaten in this country. For example, American researchers know how to produce soy flour products that greatly improve both the quality and the nutrition of baked goods like cakes, cookies, doughnuts, breads, and crackers. The addition of 12 percent soy flour inexpensively increases the protein level of a baked product by approximately 50 percent. But soy flour is not being used. An executive staff member at the Archer Daniels Midland Company, an innovator in the production of new soy products, admitted that, "There is a great deal of pressure not to produce and sell soy products in America. The largest problem we face is the fact that the heavy beef states provide active resistance to the increased use of soy products. Precisely because soy has more protein than meat and is far less expensive and more efficient, powerful meat councils lobby to prevent its use and to maintain meat levels."

They do that in part by making 90 percent of the unexported soy supply in this country unavailable to the American public. Instead of being sold to people who need it, this food, which could fill the awful, crying everyday need of starving men, women, and children, is used as animal feed.

The meat councils fighting to maintain current levels of beef production do not tell the public that the amount of edible protein they feed to the animals we eat is enough to make up for the whole world's protein deficit. America's livestock are fed ten times as much edible protein as that consumed by the people of America. In fact, America's livestock are fed as much grain as the eight hundred million people of China and the six hundred million people of India, together, eat in a year.[38]

The truth, and the real outrage, is that the animals which are consuming all that grain do not even need to eat it. They have an ability that human beings do not have, an ability to survive and grow and be healthy simply by grazing on land unsuited for crops. Animals like cattle and sheep are ruminants. Their digestive tracts possess a unique fermentation process which interacts with bacteria and protozoa and produces protein from grass.

Our livestock feeding practices did not develop because the animals needed the food, they developed because the country needed to find a profitable way to get rid of its surplus supply of grain. In 1940 two-thirds of the cattle in the United States were not fed any grain. By 1972 over two-thirds were fed grain. The Department of Agriculture will quickly point out that only 25 percent of the feed these animals consume today is grain. That is correct, but that 25 percent represents the bulk of our expendable grain supply and it represents enough grain to feed the hungry of the *entire world.*

The main effect on the animals themselves is simply more fat, most of which people trim and throw away before the animal is eaten. Despite this, the Department of Agriculture carefully supports the system. It gives the highest rating to and permits the most money to be charged for the animals that have the most marbled fat. What the consumer who buys meat is actually getting is more cholesterol, more calories, less protein, and higher prices. It is not in their economic interest and it's not even good for them. The primary difference in livestock that are not fed grain is a slower rate of growth. If ranchers suddenly withdrew all grain from their animals feed troughs, it would significantly reduce America's current meat supply. However, many agronomists believe that several other options exist that would allow us to free much or all of that grain for starving human beings and still produce the same amount of beef, if that were our priority.

Dr. Harlow Hodgson, an agronomist at the Agricultural Experiment Station at the University of Wisconsin and one of the country's leading experts, put it this way: "If we had to produce livestock without using any grain at all, my feeling is we could do it and still produce as much meat as we do now. Most ruminant nutritionists and people who understand forages agree with me. Of course we would need to produce more forage per acre, and forage that had higher energy content. We would have to eliminate losses during the harvesting process but it could be done. All it would really take is a decision to do it."

America's beef raising methods waste more than food. They use eight times as much water as growing vegetables and grains. It takes at least ten thousand pounds of water to produce every pound of grain-fed beef. An acre of land used to raise steer produces about one pound of protein. That same acre could provide seventeen pounds of protein if it were planted with soybeans.

To imagine what this means in practical, everyday terms, picture yourself at a restaurant in front of an eight-ounce steak and then imagine the room filled with forty-five to fifty people with empty bowls in front of them. For the feed costs of your steak, each of their bowls could be filled with a cup of soybeans or cooked grain.[39]

Some Americans claim that the problem is one of distribution and that it would continue no matter what the supply. Distributing food to the hungry has been a problem. Preserving food and transporting it where poor roads or no roads exist have added to the difficulty. But the process of dehydrating and freeze-drying foods does a lot toward reducing the difficulties of transportation. It also reduces required storage space by 80 percent and protects against rats, insects, and spoilage for up to twenty years.

Dr. Jean Mayer, former Harvard nutritionist and member of the President's Commission on World Hunger, estimated that reducing meat production by just 10 percent would release enough grain to feed sixty million people. The late Hubert Humphrey urged Americans to eat one less hamburger a week so that ten million tons of grain would be made available to hungry people each year. Former Secretary of Agriculture Earl Butz objected to suggestions that we cut back on our own meat production and consumption to meet the food needs of others. "Americans are not going to eat one less hamburger per week," he said. "They are going to eat one more hamburger per week and, furthermore, they need have no sense of guilt."

Actually, we do not need to eat less meat to free American grain for human consumption, we could simply feed the animals less grain or *no* grain.

Experts estimate that if American cattlemen would let their herds graze for just *two* extra weeks on the open range and then bring them into the feed lots, by that process alone, enough grain could be saved to feed *all* the hungry in the world.[40]

It comes to this: The average steer unnecessarily consumes four thousand pounds of grain a year. Some of that grain could be used to create an emergency grain reserve for the United States, which could provide food for hungry Americans, offset any food crisis caused by energy disruptions, and allow dangerous chemicals that increase productivity to be abandoned. The rest of the grain, with some hard logistic work and effort, could provide food for the starving all over the world. Not *instead* of having them improve their own methods of food production but to keep them alive until they are able to. Clearly there would need to be a way for farmers to sell the grain at a fair price and there would need to be new methods of distribution, but I believe it could be done. It took 10 years, 20,000 contractors, 300,000 technicians, and $24 billion to put a man on the moon. Surely, if we redirected that kind of time, talent, money, and effort we could feed the hungry in America and the countless millions in other countries whose survival depends on our judgment.

However, since World War II the national policy in America actually has been to decrease research on how to gain maximum animal growth rates without soybeans and other grains. Instead, we have said we have more important ways to spend our money.

Dr. Paul Putnam, director of the Agriculture Department's Beltsville, Maryland, Research Center, points out that sugar beet tops, citrus pulp, tankage matter left from slaughtered animals, grain mash left from distilling alcohol, apple pomice, whey left from making butter and cheese, high nitrite animal wastes, and even cellulose fibers from newsprint and sawdust could be fed to animals instead of grain.

A study by the American Forage and Grassland Council reports that in the United States enough rough forage is left unused on seventy-five million acres of corn and sorghum stalks after the grain has been harvested to feed between twelve million and thirty million additional head of beef cows annually.[41]

Dr. Harlow Hodgson also predicts that if we simply supplemented the animals' diet with these currently wasted corn and sorghum stalks we could immediately reduce the grain we feed to our livestock *without* reducing our meat output at all.

Nature created a system through which forage can be converted into protein for us by ruminant animals, making it possible for people to use this massive supply of food. But in America the economic interests of a few have caused an almost incomprehensible amount of waste. That waste has, in turn, caused massive suffering and needless starvation. The protein wasted in the U.S. alfalfa crop alone is equivalent to more than half the total annual protein requirement of the entire American population.

Right now there are thousands of acres of grasslands in the Southeastern and Eastern states that are idle because there has been no incentive to use them for grazing cattle and sheep. In fact, 63 percent of America's total land area is classified as grazing land. If farmers and ranchers would simply use that land for grazing along with available, currently wasted supplements, beef production would continue uninterrupted and there would be enough available grain to end starvation not just in America but in the world.

In order to confirm that such a possibility actually existed and was being ignored, and in order to see for myself a country where it was working and learn firsthand what the problems associated with it were, I traveled to Australia. I found that techniques currently being used in that country with great success suggest that, in addition to saving the grain to feed the hungry, America could also restore much of its badly damaged soil, reduce erosion, and diminish the need for chemical fertilizers.

Virtually all Australian beef is raised without any grain at all. Australia has far less of a resource base than America; much of its land is desert. Even in the grain-growing areas, soil fertility and rainfall are not as good as ours. The margin for error is lower. As one Australian farmer astutely put it, "Australia began with a desert, America is creating one."

Up until the late 1930s South Australia's grain zone had been exploited by extensive farming much as ours is now. The soil's natural fertility was being destroyed, soil erosion was acute, salinity was developing, crop yields had stopped increasing. South Australian agricultural experts knew that maintenance of the land was vital. They knew that they could not survive without the land and what grew on it, and so they began to search for answers.

The technique they settled on integrates grain and livestock production. It is very simple. Each farmer rotates cereal crops with forage crops. The forage crops used in Australia are legumes. The legumes provide all of the food the livestock need to eat. At the same time they prevent erosion and allow the soil that has been taken out of grain production to restore itself. The legumes also increase the nitrogen content of the soil and decrease the need for chemical fertilizers.

Typically, Australian farms are family farms. Roughly half of each farmer's land is devoted to grain. The other half to legumes. Each year, the farmer moves his livestock to the area that he has taken out of grain production and planted with the soil-restoring animal feed.

According to Henry Day, chief agronomist with the South Australian Department of Agriculture, in 1978 and 1979 Australian grain harvests were record-breaking, and, in 1980 even those records were topped. Soil erosion was minimal. Dependence on petrochemicals had been reduced. Very little nitrogen fertilizer was needed, and no irrigation systems were used. Instead, Australians had developed drought-resistant varieties of grain. In addition, so much beef was being raised without any grain at all that only a fraction was being consumed by the Australian population; more than 80 percent was exported.

Teams of technicians plan to try the Australian technique in Algeria, Tasmania, Libya, Iraq, Jordan, and Morocco. When I asked chief agronomist Henry Day if he thought such a system could also be used in the United States, he looked surprised. "Well, yes," he said, "it could. Various strains of legumes could be adapted to America's climatic needs; your beef could certainly be raised on legumes and without grain. But we've always been told that you people had the best of everything, that your soil fertility was good, your production was excellent, and you people were well fed. We've been told that your agricultural system was the wonder of the modern world."

"Yes, we've been told the same thing," I said, and I thanked him.

You can't find a grain-supplied feedlot in southern Australia, since virtually all beef is processed on improved grasses and legumes. The legumes grow slowly through the winter and prevent erosion. In the spring they grow quickly and the animals start to put on weight. During the summer the legumes dry out because there is almost no rain in Australia. The dry legumes maintain the animals through most of the summer. Typically, the animals are slaughtered when they are about ten months old, at weaning, so most of the fat they get comes from the mother's milk. "Of course you realize," Richard Williams, beef production manager for the South Australian Department of Agriculture, explained, "we save a tremendous amount of grain, but there isn't much marbleized fat on our meat. I've never been to America or eaten American beef, but I've heard Americans probably would not be satisfied with Australian beef. I'm told that our beef is drier, and that it doesn't have the same amount of flavor."

That night I went to a restaurant and I ordered one of the least expensive dinners on the menu—a steak. I took my first curious bite of the huge steak that was placed in front of me, expecting shoe leather. To my surprise, it tasted as good as any meat I had ever eaten in America. I couldn't tell the difference.

Clearly, then, there are ways to get more food from both the sea and the land. We are starving people *needlessly*. We are also destroying our land and in the process we are irreparably damaging the country in ways that will soon create real food scarcity.

And yet it seems that the policymakers of America still genuinely do not understand where the country is heading or even that if enough people go hungry there will come a point before apathy and death when violence, born out of deep need, will erupt.

When the Great Depression of the thirties brought hunger on a scale never before known in the United States, food riots spread from city to city. Even as Roosevelt's New Deal sought to come to grips with the problem, hungry Virginia miners smashed shop windows, looting food. Jobless auto workers in Detroit invaded grocery stores, filled their baskets with food, and fought their way out. In Arkansas, sharecroppers marched on a general store and stripped the shelves of all its food. When President Roosevelt put Harry L. Hopkins at the head of the Federal Emergency Relief Administration, Hopkins gave one curt order to the FERA officials. He said, "Feed the hungry, and goddamn fast!"[42]

Today, we do not have that kind of a new deal. Instead, the American government and Department of Agriculture are pandering to destructive short-term corporate interests. For a long time the land produced, almost defiantly, despite abuse. For decades energy was made available and inflation was kept under control. But now, inevitably, the destruction, the exploitation, and the waste are coming full circle. If they continue and the people of this country do nothing, no one will be safe.

America has the technology to make the changes but it needs to reorient its thinking. It needs to reestablish a sense of community and a sense of common destiny. America needs to make decisions based on its long-term interests, not on four-year election cycles. Those decisions should be in harmony with each other, with nature, and with the laws that transcend short-term interests. We can still combine the best of our old values with the best of our new skills, and create a new level of richness.

Our agriculture is part of our total culture. It cannot be dealt with in isolation. It cannot remain intact unless the related crises of energy abuse, inflation, land abuse, and human abuse are also resolved. Those crises will require many changes of us, but they will also offer new opportunities. If Americans make the changes unwillingly, not many will be made and each one will be seen as a form of deprivation. But if this becomes a time of cooperation and sharing, each person can make an enormous difference.

Mother Teresa, the Nobel Prize-winning nun and caretaker of Calcutta's poor, once said, "Never miss the opportunity of giving until it hurts." Some of us will have that opportunity.

Many things have changed in America since the day in 1974 when I found eighty-four-year old Martha Roca starving.

The United States is less resilient now. We have less time. We can no longer afford to wait passively for improvement or to hope that the government will take care of things. We must overcome our own powerlessness. The first step toward doing that is recognizing the problems that we face. For each of us that process is different.

It was Martha Roca who first enabled me to make the connection between the human suffering and the official statistics. It was through her that I came to understand that someone in Philadelphia was actually starving, and later, that millions of people, all over America, were hungry.

My outrage at that suffering in the midst of affluence compelled me to look further and discover the material that forms the substance of this book. I never had a chance to thank Mrs. Roca for helping me to make the connections or for teaching me that what each of us does or fails to do even on the smallest scale does make a difference.

Back in 1974 after my first hunger article was published, many organizations had rushed to her aid.

I visited and brought food a few days after the article appeared. When I arrived at her house I found that she was receiving hot lunches. Somehow, she was convinced that they were coming from me.

"Do you like the lunches?" I had asked.

"Oh, yes, thank you, thank you very much. Wonderful. How can I ever thank you enough?"

"Do you eat any other meal besides this one?"

"Oh, yes, I eat everything."

"I know that, but do you get another meal at night?" I asked.

"I get very hungry at night," she said. Then, leaning heavily on a chair to support her weak legs, Mrs. Roca took me into the kitchen, opened her refrigerator, and proudly showed me all of the empty paper plates and paper cups from each finished lunch, neatly arranged inside.

After I left, I made several calls to see if she could get an evening meal delivered. It seemed promising. Several organizations told me they thought it would be possible. Then, rather suddenly, I became busy with public response, with traveling, and with writing other articles. I stopped taking her food. I did not know that everyone involved would assume, as I had assumed, that someone else was taking care of her.

Some months later, on a cold Saturday morning, I returned, carrying a bag of groceries. As I walked toward Mrs. Roca's house I realized how much I had missed her. I could already imagine her opening the door, laughing with pleasure, and saying "Hello, darling dear" as she saw me. When I began providing her with food, I did not realize that she was also providing me with something I very much needed. I knocked on the battered old door, supporting the bag on my knee. There was no answer. I knew she had to be home. She never went out, never went anywhere, for fear that the neighborhood boys would attack her. I knocked louder.

Maybe she's visiting next door, I told myself. I went to the next house and rang the bell. A heavyset woman peeked out of the window then opened the door.

"I'm looking for Martha Roca," I said.

The woman looked at the groceries, then at me; her eyes grew softer, almost apologetic. "I'm sorry, lady, but you're too late. They carried her out of there last week. If I'd known she needed food I would have brought her something, I really would." Her voice drifted off. "I never heard a sound from her. She never asked me for any help. She just starved to death right in her bed."

Through Martha Roca's death I learned that the strongest component in what we have failed to do in America, and in what we can do, is the human component. The answers will come from the action that each of us takes and the responsibilities that each of us assumes. It means not forgetting as I forgot. It means not allowing our neighbors to forget. It means reaching our political leaders. It means implementing things and having the discipline, the judgment, and the strength of purpose to follow them until they are accomplished. The options are still ours. We can care for ourselves, each other, and the earth together OR we can destroy what is left.

Notes

1. Myron Winick, ed., and Martha Osnos, trans., *Hunger Disease Studies by The Jewish Physicians in the Warsaw Ghetto* (New York, 1979), pp. 14-15.
2. Winick, *Hunger Disease*
3. "Report of the Advisory Council on Social Security," *Commissioner's Bulletin SSA*, no. 15 (December 15, 1980), p. 2.
4. Howard Ruff, *How to Prosper During the Coming Bad Years* (New York, 1979), p. 53.
5. Ruff, *How to Prosper*, p. 57.
6. Robert Kennedy, speech at Valparaiso University, Valparaiso, Indiana, 1968.
7. Vernon Loch, "Food Aid in Trouble," *The Philadelphia Inquirer*, August 3, 1980.
8. Iver Petersen, "Inflation Compelling the Middle Income People to Ask for Public Aid," *The New York Times*, April 20, 1980, p. 1.
9. Richard E. Nicholls, *Beginning Hydroponics* (Phila.,: Running Press, 1977) p.20.
10. Harold Saber, "Census Counts Your Farms in the New York Area," *The New York Times*, August 17, 1980, p. 29.
11. Steinhart and Steinhart, *Perspectives on Energy*, p. 61.
12. Norma Jean Skjold, "Nitrates: An Insoluble Problem?" *New Land Review*, Fall 1977, p. 10.
13. Steinhart and Steinhart, *Perspectives on Energy*, p. 61.
14. Donald L. Bartlett and James B. Steele, Energy Anarchy Series, *The Philadelphia Inquirer*, December 9-13, 1980.
15. Ibid.
16. Ibid.

17. Lester R. Brown, *The Politics and Responsibility of the North American Breadbasket*, Worldwatch Paper 2 (Washington, D.C., 1975), p. 1.
18. Robert McCartney, "Third World Food Crisis," *The Philadelphia Inquirer*, November 11, 1979.
19. "Toward a Troubled 21st Century," *Time*, August 4, 1980, p. 54.
20. Ibid.
21. *Alternatives for Completing the Tellico Dam Project*, TVA, p. 10.
22. S. David Freeman, chairman, Tennessee Valley Authority, statement to Subcommittee on Fisheries, Wildlife Conservation and the Environment, U.S. House of Representatives, June 23, 1978.
23. George Anthan, "Feeding Our Hungry World from Less and Less Farmland," *Des Moines Register*, July 8, 1979.
24. D. Pimentel et al., "Land Degradation: Effects on Food and Energy Resources," *Science*, October 8, 1976, p. 150.
25. Ibid.
26. Eddie Albert, "Civilization Rests on Topsoil," *The Mother Earth News*, May–June 1980, p. 68.
27. George Anthan, "Land People Trends Hint at Food Disaster," *Des Moines Register*, July 9, 1979.
28. Ronald B. Taylor, "Herbicides Hot Dispute Stirs Oregon," *Los Angeles Times*, December 30, 1979; reprinted in "The Poisoning of America," Part II, pp. 26–29.
29. Charles F. Wurster, *The New York Times*, May 29, 1979, sec. A, p. 18.
30. Anthony Decrosta and Dan Looker, *Pesticides and Your Health* (Emmaus, PA), p. 31.
31. Ronald B. Taylor, "Cattle Deaths Stir Pesticide Debate," *Los Angeles Times*, November 5, 1979; reprinted in "The Poisoning of America," Part II, pp. 16–20.
32. Ibid., p. 19.
33. William Tucker, "The Next American Dustbowl," *Atlantic Monthly*, July 1979, p. 21.
34. Robert Van den Bosch, from speech delivered to Society for Occupational and Environmental Health, quoted in *Food Monitor*, January– February, 1979, p. 23.
35. J. I. Rodale, *Food Monitor*, January–February 1979, p. 274.
36. Rachel Carson, *Silent Spring* (New York, 1962), p. 18.
37. Mike Feinsilber, *The Philadelphia Inquirer*, December 24, 1980.
38. Jules Archer, *Hunger on Planet Earth* (New York, 1977), p. 178.
39. American Friends Service Committee, *Taking Charge* (New York, 1977), p. 274.
40. Frances Moore Lappe, *Diet for a Small Planet* (New York, 1975), p. 14.
41. Archer, *Hunger*, p. 171.
42. Harlow Hodgson, "We Won't Need to Eliminate Beef Cattle," *Crop and Soils Magazine*, November 1974, p. 9.
43. Archer, *Hunger*, p. 130.

Bibliography

Alperovitz, Gar, and Faux, Jeff. "Building a Democratic Economy." Reprinted from *The Progressive*, n.d.

Archer, Jules. *Hunger on Planet Earth*. New York: Thomas Y. Crowell Co., 1977.

Bagdikian, Ben H. *In the Midst of Plenty*. Boston: Beacon Press, 1964.

Barr, Jeri. "What? Hunger in My Town?" *Food Monitor*, January-February 1979, pp. 4-7.

Bartlett, Donald L., and Steele, James B. "Energy Anarchy." Series of articles in *The Philadelphia Inquirer*, December 9-13, 1980.

Belden, Joe, and Forte, Gregg. *Toward a National Food Policy*. Washington, DC: Exploratory Project for Economic Alternatives, 1976.

Berry, Wendell. *The Unsettling of America Culture and Agriculture*. New York: Avon, 1979.

Birch, Herbert G. "Functional Effects of Fetal Malnutrition." *Hospital Practice*, March 1971, pp. 134-136, 141-148.

———. *Malnutrition, Learning, and Intelligence*. Washington, DC: Department of Health, Education, and Welfare, DHEW Publication No. (05) 73-96.

Biswas, Margaret R, and Biswas, Asit K. *Food, Climate, and Man*. New York: John Wiley and Sons, 1979.

Bohn, Carey, ed. *Survival in a Crisis*. Minneapolis: Investment Rarities, 1979.

229

Braver, Ruth C. *A Final Project on the Chicago Nutrition Program for Older Adults.* Chicago: Mayor's Office for Senior Citizens, January 1972.

Brown, Harrison. *The Human Future Revisited: The World Predicament and Possible Solutions.* New York: W.W. Norton and Co., Inc., 1978.

Brown, Kevin. "Presidential Commission Up-Date." *Food Monitor,* January–February 1979, p. 19.

Brown, Lester. "Food Versus Fuel: Competing Uses for Cropland." *Environment,* May 1980, pp. 32–40.

———. "Global Economic Ills: The Worst May Be Yet to Come." *The Futurist,* June 1978, pp. 157–168.

———. *The Global Economic Prospect: New Sources of Economic Stress.* Washington, DC: Worldwatch Institute, 1978. (Worldwatch Paper 20.)

———. "A Harvest of Neglect: The World's Declining Cropland." *The Futurist,* April 1979, pp. 141–151.

———. *The Politics and Responsibility of the North American Breadbasket.* Washington, DC: Worldwatch Institute, 1975 (Worldwatch Paper 2.)

———. *World Without Borders.* New York: Vintage Books, 1973.

Brown, Lester R., and Eckholm, Erik P. *By Bread Alone.* New York: Praeger Publishers, 1974.

Brown, Michael H. *Laying Waste: The Poisoning of America By Toxic Chemicals.* New York: Pantheon Books, 1979.

Carson, Rachel. *Silent Spring.* Greenwich, CT: Fawcett Publications, Inc., 1962.

Center for Rural Affairs. *Wheels of Fortune. A Report on the Impact of Center Pivot Irrigation on the Ownership of Land in Nebraska.* Walthill, NB: Center for Rural Affairs, 1976.

Center for Science in the Public Interest. *99 Ways to a Simple Lifestyle.* New York: Anchor Books, 1976.

Chamber of Commerce of the United States. "The Changing Structure of U.S. Agribusiness and Its contributions to the National Economy." Paper produced by the Chamber of Commerce, Washington, DC,1974.

Chapin, James B. "What Americans Think About Hunger." *Food Monitor,* May–June 1980, pp. 18–19.

Children's Foundation. WIC Advocacy Staff. *Working for Women and Children First.* Washington, DC: Children's Foundation, 1975.

Commoner, Barry. *The Politics of Energy.* New York: Alfred A. Knopf, 1979.

———. *The Poverty of Power.* New York: Bantam Books, 1976.

Cook, Earl. *Man, Energy, Society.* San Francisco: W.H. Freeman and Co., 1976.

Cornish, Edward. "The Great Depression of the 1980s: Could It Really Happen?" *The Futurist,* October 1979, pp. 353–380.

———. *1999: The World of Tomorrow.* Washington, DC: World Future Society, 1978.

———. *The Study of the Future.* Washington, DC: World Future Society, 1977.

230

Council on Foods and Nutrition to the AMA Board of Trustees. "Malnutrition and Hunger in the United States." *Journal of the American Medical Association*, July 13, 1970.

Cramer, Gail L., and Jensen, Clarence W. *Agricultural Economics and Agribusiness*. New York: John Wiley and Sons, 1979.

DeCrosta, Anthony, and Looker, Dan. *Pesticides and Your Health*. Emmaus, PA: Rodale Press, Inc., n.d.

Dedinsky, Mary. "Hunger in Chicago." (Update of 1969 series). *Chicago Sun-Times*, November 10-12, 1973.

Dobrin, Lyn, ed. "Critiquing the Commission." *Food Monitor*, March-April 1980, p. 5.

Eberstadt, Nick. "Myths of the Food Crisis." *The New York Review*, February 19, 1976, pp. 32-37.

Eckholm, Erik, and Record, Frank. *The Two Faces of Malnutrition*. Washington, DC: Worldwatch Institute, 1976. (Worldwatch Paper 9.)

Ehrlich, Paul. *The End of Affluence*. New York: Ballantine Books, 1974.

―――. *The Population Bomb*. New York: Ballantine Books, 1968.

Emergency Food. Reprinted from *Food Monitor* magazine, Reprint No. 2.

Enzer, Selwyn; Drobnick; Richard, and Alter, Steven. *Neither Feast Nor Famine: Food Conditions to the Year 2000*. Lexington, MA: Lexington Books, 1978.

Erhard, Werner. "An Idea Whose Time Has Come: The Hunger Project." *The Graduate Review*, 1977.

Esbenshade, Henry W. *Farming: Sources for a Social and Ecologically Accountable Agriculture*. Davis, CA: Alternative Agricultural Resources Project, 1976.

Everdel, Ros, and Frank, Maurice. "The New York City Story." *Food Monitor*, May-June 1979, p. 17.

"Feeding the World in the Year 2000." Articles reprinted from *The Futurist*.

Fleming, Virginia. *Women and Children First or Last?* Washington, D.C.: The Children's Foundation, 1975.

Fleming, Virginia; Harvey, Stefan; and Keefer, Judy. *Overcoming Malnutrition: Putting Federal Programs to Work*. Washington, DC: The Children's Foundation, 1977.

The Food Research and Action Center. *If We Had Ham, We Could Have Ham and Eggs ... If We Had Eggs*. Yonkers, NY: Gazette Press, Inc., 1972.

Ford, Barbara. *Future Food Alternate Protein For the Year 2000*. New York: William Morrow and Co., Inc., 1978.

Gabel, Medard. *Ho-ping: Food for Everyone*. New York: Anchor Books, 1979.

Galbraith, John Kenneth. *The Nature of Mass Poverty*. London: Harvard University Press, 1979.

Garson, Barbara. "The Bottle Baby Scandal: Milking the Third World for All It's Worth." *Mother Jones*, December 1977.

Gaylin, Willard; Glasser, Ira; Marcus, Steven; et al. *Doing Good*. New York: Pantheon Books, 1978.

Goldschmidt, Walter. *As You Sow*. Montclair, NJ: Allanheld, Osmun and Co., 1978.

"Grain Becomes a Weapon." *Time*, January 21, 1980, pp. 12-16, 21-22.

Gribbin, John. *Forecasts, Famines and Freezes*. New York: Walker and Co., 1976.

Halbert, Frederic, and Halbert, Sandra. *Bitter Harvest*. Grand Rapids, MI: William B. Eerdmans Publishing Co., 1978.

Hall, Ross Hume. "The Changing American Diet: Can Our Cells Cope With It?" *Food Monitor*, January-February 1980, pp. 17-18.

Harrington, Michael. *The Other America*. Baltimore: Penguin Books Inc., 1962.

Harris, Michael. "Eating Oil: From the Kitchens of Amoco Comes Petroleum Protein, the New 'Natural' Food." Mother Jones, August 1977, pp. 1-4.

Hellman, Hal. *Feeding the World of the Future*. New York: M. Evans and Company, Inc., 1972.

Henderson, Carter. *The Inevitability of Petroleum Rationing in the United States*. Princeton, NJ: Princeton Center for Alternative Futures, Inc., 1978.

Hill and Knowlton, Inc. "H&K World Food Crisis Memorandum—No. 1." Report of an H&K World Food Crisis Task Force, September 3, 1974.

Hinchey, Maurice. "What About Us?" *Food Monitor*, March-April 1980, pp. 12-13.

Hodgson, Harlow J. "Food from Plant Products—Forage." Paper presented at A Symposium on the Complementary Role of Plant and Animal Products in the U.S. Food System, November 29-30, 1977, National Academy of Sciences, Washington, DC.

———. "Forage Crops." *Scientific American*, February 1976, pp. 60-68, 74-75.

———. "Forage Research Has Taken a Back Seat . . ." *Hoards' Dairyman*, May 10, 1977, pp. 589-591, 599-600.

———. "Forages and Food." Talk presented at Certified Alfalfa Seed Council Forum, March 18, 1980, Chicago, IL.

———. "Forages, Ruminant Livestock, and Food." *BioScience*, October 1976, pp. 625-630.

———. "Gaps in Knowledge and Technology for Finishing Cattle on Forages." *Journal of Animal Science*, 1977, pp. 896-900.

———. "Man's Benefactor." *Nutrition Today*, March-April 1979, pp. 16-25.

———. "Our Industry Today: Role of the Dairy Cow in World Food Production." *Journal of Dairy Science*, February 1979, pp. 343-351.

———. "Potential Increases in Food Through Forage and Animal Production." Paper presented at Northeast Branch Meeting, American Society of Agronomy, June 27-29, 1977, Burlington, VT.

———. "The Role of Forage in Food Production." Paper presented at 22nd Farm Seed Conference, November 16, 1976, Kansas City, MO.

Hodin, Jay. *Malnutrition and Developmental Disabilities—A Causal Relationship*. n.p.: Illinois Association for Retarded Citizens, 1975.

Interreligious Taskforce on U.S. Food Policy. "Multinational Corporations and Global Development." *Hunger*, No. 24, July 1980. (Published by National Impact, Washington, DC.)

Jegen, Mary Evelyn, and Wilber, Charles. *Growth With Equity*. New York: Paulist Press, 1979.

Kirsch, Jeff, and Lipner, Jay. *Frac's Guide to the Food Stamp Program*. New York: Food Research and Action Center, 1975.

Komisar, Lucy. *Down and Out in the USA.* New York: Franklin Watts, Inc., 1973.

Kotz, Nick. *Hunger in America: The Federal Response.* New York: The Field Foundation, 1979.

———. *Let Them Eat Promises.* New York: Doubleday and Co., Inc., 1971.

Kramer, Mark. *Making Milk, Meat and Money from the American Soil.* Boston: Little, Brown and Co., 1977.

Lappe, Frances Moore. *Diet for a Small Planet.* New York: Ballantine Books, 1975.

Lappe, Frances Moore, and Collins, Joseph. *Food First.* Boston: Houghton Mifflin Co., 1977.

———. "The World Bank and the Hungry: Don't Bank on It." *Food Monitor,* May–June 1979, pp. 4–7.

Lasch, Christopher. *The Culture of Narcissism.* New York: W.W. Norton and Co., Inc., 1978.

Leghorn, Lisa, and Roodkowsky, Mary. *Who Really Starves? Women and World Hunger.* New York: Friendship Press, 1977.

Leonard, Rodney E. "No Program, No Plan." *Food Monitor,* March–April 1980, pp. 16–17.

Lerza, Catherine. "U.S. Farmers Ignored—Again." *Food Monitor,* March–April 1980, pp. 6–7.

Lerza, Catherine, and Jacobson, Catherine. *Food for People Not for Profit.* New York: Ballantine Books, 1975.

MacKay, Wray. "Advocates for the Hungry." *Food Monitor,* May–June 1979, p. 16.

———. "Hotline How-To." *Food Monitor,* May–June 1979, p. 18.

McLaughlin, Martin M. *The United States and World Development Agenda 1979.* New York: Praeger Publishers, 1978.

Marien, Michael, editor. *Future Survey Annual, 1979. A Guide to the Recent Literature of Trends, Forecasts, and Policy Proposals.* Washington, DC: World Future Society, 1980.

Meador, Roy. *Future Energy Alternatives.* Ann Arbor, MI: Ann Arbor Science Publishers, Inc., 1978.

Meadows, Donella H.; Meadows, Denis L.; Randers, Jorgen; et al. *The Limits to Growth.* New York: Signet Books, 1972.

Mesarovic, Minajlo, and Pestel, Edward. *Mankind at the Turning Point.* New York: Signet Books, 1974.

Miles, Rufus E., Jr. *Awakening from the American Dream.* New York: Universe Books, 1976.

Morgan, Dan. *Merchants of Grain.* New York: Viking Press, 1979.

Moss, N. Henry, and Mayer, Jean, eds. *Food and Nutrition in Health and Disease.* Annals of The New York Academy of Sciences. Volume 300. New York: New York Academy of Sciences, 1977.

Murphy, Maureen, and Span, Paula. *Needless Hunger: A Report on the School Breakfast Program in Philadelphia.* Philadelphia: Philadelphia Jaycees, 1975.

Myrdal, Gunnar. *The Challenge of World Poverty.* New York: Pantheon Books, 1970.

Nelson, Jack A. *Hunger for Justice: The Politics of Food and Faith.* Maryknoll, NY: Orbis Books, 1980.

Ophuls, William. *Ecology and the Politics of Scarcity.* San Francisco: W.H. Freeman and Co., 1977.

Paddock, William, and Paddock, Paul. *Famine—1975!* Boston: Little, Brown and Co., 1967.

Page, Louise. *A Guide to Menu Planning, Buying, and the Care of Food for Community Programs.* Washington, DC: U.S. Department of Agriculture, 1972.

Peccei, Aurelio. "The World We Are Leaving Our Children." *World Future Society Bulletin,* March-April 1979, pp. 6-9.

Pelcovits, Jeanette. "Nutrition for Older Americans." *Journal of the American Dietetic Association,* January 1971, pp. 17-21.

Phillips, Owen. *The Last Chance Energy Book.* Baltimore: The Johns Hopkins University Press, 1979.

The Poisoning of America. Series of articles reprinted from the *Los Angeles Times,* June 28, 1979.

The Poisoning of America, Part II. Series of articles reprinted from the *Los Angeles Times,* September 24, 1979.

Quirk, William J. "Why the Government Prefers Inflation." *Business and Society Review,* n.d., pp. 42-46.

Rockey, Linda. "Hunger in Chicago: Officially It Doesn't Exist." Reprinted from the *Chicago Sun-Times,* April 1969.

Ruedisili, Lon C., and Firebaugh, Morris W. *Perspectives on Energy.* New York: Oxford University Press, 1975.

Ruff, Howard. *How to Prosper During the Coming Bad Years.* New York: Times Books, 1979.

Scarpa, Ioannis S., and Kiefer, Helen Chilton. *Sourcebook on Food and Nutrition.* Chicago: Marquis Academic Media, 1978.

Schwartz, Loretta. "Boston's Seduced and Hungry: Abandoned?" *Boston,* September 1976, pp. 83-84, 117-124.

———. "Hungry Women in America." *Ms.,* October 1977, pp. 60-63, 102, 106-107.

———. "Nothing to Eat." *Philadelphia,* December 1974, pp. 178-192.

———. "Nothing to Eat." *The Washingtonian,* November 1975, pp. 92-99, 253.

———. "People Are Starving in Chicago." *Chicago,* June 1976, pp. 92-99.

———. "The Plight of America's Five Million Migrants." *Ms.,* June 1978, pp. 65-71.

———. "Uranium Deaths at Crown Point." *Ms.,* October 1979, pp. 53-54, 59, 81-82.

Simon, Arthur. *Bread for the World.* New York: Paulist Press, 1975.

———. *Breaking Bread With the Hungry.* Minneapolis, MN: Augsburg Publishing House, 1971.

Simple Living Collective American Friends Service Committee. *Taking Charge.* New York: Bantam Books, 1975.

Sinclair, John C., and Saigal, Saroj. "Nutritional Influences in Industrial Societies." *American Journal of Diseases of Children,* May 1975, pp. 549-554.

Slater, R. Giuseppi; Kitt, Doug; Widelock, Dave; et al. *The Earth Belongs to the People: Ecology and Power.* New York: Peoples Press, 1970.

Steinhart, John S., and Steinhart, Carol. *Perspectives on Energy.* New York: Oxford, 1975.

Stobaugh, Robert, and Yergin, Daniel, eds. *Energy Future.* New York: Random House, 1979.

234

Sullivan, William G. and Claycombe, W. Wayne. *Fundamentals of Forecasting*. Reston, VA: Reston Publishing Co., Inc., 1977.

Tamarkin, Bob. "The Growth Industry." *Forbes*, March 2, 1981, pp. 90-94.

Tennessee Valley Authority. *Alternatives for Completing the Tellico Project*. Knoxville, TN: TVA, 1978.

—— . *Environmental Statement*. *Tellico Project*, Vol. II. Knoxville, TN: TVA, n.d.

"Text of Reagan's State of Union Message on Economic Recovery." *The New York Times*, February 19, 1981, p. B8.

Tuve, George. *Energy, Environment, Populations, and Food*. New York: John Wiley and Sons, 1976.

U.S. Comptroller General. Report to the Congress. *World Hunger and Malnutrition Continue: Slow Progress in Carrying Out World Food Conference Objectives*. Washington, DC: U.S. General Accounting Office, No. ID-80-12, January 11, 1980.

U.S. Congress (House). *A Bill to Amend the National School Lunch and Child Nutrition Acts . . .*, H.R. 4222, 94th Congress, 1st session, 1975.

—— . Committee on Agriculture. Subcommittee on Domestic Marketing, Consumer Relations, and Nutrition. *Nutrition Education: National Consumer Nutrition Information Act of 1978*. Hearings on H.R. 11761 and H.R. 12428, Part 1 and 2. 95th Congress, 1st and 2nd sessions, 1977 and 1978.

—— . *National School Lunch Act and Child Nutrition Act of 1966 Amendments of 1975*. Report to Accompany H.R. 4222. 94th Congress, 1st session, 1975, H. Rept. 94-427.

U.S. Congress. Office of Technology Assessment. *Nutrition Research Alternatives*. Washington, DC: Superintendent of Documents, 1978.

U.S. Congress (Senate). *National School Lunch Act and Child Nutrition Act of 1966 Amendments of 1975*. Report on H.R. 4222. 94th Congress, 1st session, 1975, S. Rept. 94-259.

—— . Select Committee on Nutrition and Human Needs. *"Hunger"* 1973 and Press Reaction. 93rd Congress, 1st session, 1973.

—— . *Implementation and Status of the Special Supplemental Food Program for Women, Infants, and Children*. 93rd Congress, 2nd session, 1974.

—— . *Index to Publications on Nutrition and Human Needs*, 93rd Congress 94th Congress, 1st session, 1975.

—— . *Report on Nutrition and Special Groups: Appendix B to Part I— Food Stamps*. 94th Congress, 1st session, 1975.

—— . *School Food Program Needs—1975*. State School Food Service Director's Response: A Working Paper. 94th Congress, 1st session, 1975.

—— . *To Save the Children: Nutritional Intervention Through Supplemental Feeding*. 93rd Congress, 2nd session, 1974.

U.S. Department of Agriculture. *Global Food Assessment, 1980*. Washington, DC: USDA, 1980.

U.S. General Accounting Office. "Changing Character and Structure of American Agriculture: An Overview." Washington, DC: GAO, No. CED-78-178, September 26, 1978.

235

Walton, Clarence C., ed. *Inflation and National Survival.* Proceedings of the Academy of Political Science, Vol. 33, No. 3. New York: Academy of Political Science, 1979.

Watkin, Donald M., and Mann, George V., eds. "Symposium: Nutrition and Aging." Proceedings of the Sessions on Nutrition and Aging at the 25th Annual Scientific Meeting of the Gerontological Society, December 17-21, 1972, San Juan, Puerto Rico. Published by U.S. Department of Health, Education, and Welfare, DHEW Publication No. (OHD) 75-20240.

Webber, Glyn, and Williams, Gill. *Ley Farming in South Australia.* South Australia: Department of Agriculture and Fisheries, n.d. (Bulletin no. 15/77).

Wedin, W.F.; Hodgson, H.G.; and Jacobson, N.L. "Utilizing Plant and Animal Resources in Producing Human Food." *Journal of Animal Science,* 1975, pp. 667-686.

Wilbur, Vincent P. "Presidential Commission Up-Date—The Hunger Commission's Preliminary Report: A Good Start But Still Incomplete." *Food Monitor,* January-February 1980, pp. 15-16.

Winick, Myron, ed. *Hunger Disease: Studies by the Jewish Physicians in the Warsaw Ghetto.* Translated by Martha Osnos. New York: John Wiley and Sons, 1979.

Winrock International Livestock Research and Training Center. *The Role of Ruminants in Support of Man.* Morrilton, AR: Winrock International, 1978.

Index

240

Printed in the United States
811700003B